MORE THAN PETTICOATS SERIES

MORE THAN PETTICOATS

REMARKABLE NEW MEXICO WOMEN

Beverly West

D1571237

TWODOT

An imprint of The Globe Pequot Press
Guilford, Connecticut

A · TWODOT · BOOK

TwoDot is a registered trademark of The Globe Pequot Press.

Cover photo: Mabel Dodge Luhan, Frieda Lawrence, and artist Dorothy Brett (left to right). Courtesy Yale Collection of American Literature, Beinecke Rare Book and Manuscript Library.

Text design: Cyndee Peil

Library of Congress Cataloging-in-Publication Data:

West, Beverly, 1961-
    More than petticoats: remarkable New Mexico women / by Beverly West.--1st ed.
        p.cm.-- (More than petticoats series)
    Includes bibliographical references and index.
    ISBN 0-7627-1222-8
    1. Women--New Mexico--Biography. 2. Women--New Mexico--History. 3. New Mexico--Biography. I. Title. II. Series.

CT3260. W47 2001
920.72'09789--dc21
                                                            2001033394

Manufactured in the United States of America
First Edition/First Printing

 Text pages printed on recycled paper.

To remarkable women everywhere
who refuse to mind their manners.

ONTENTS

ACKNOWLEDGMENTS
vii

INTRODUCTION
ix

MOTHER MAGDALEN AND THE SISTERS OF LORETTO
Pioneers of Education
1

NAMPEYO (SNAKE THAT DOES NOT BITE)
Hopi Master Potter
12

MARY COLTER
Architect of the Earth
23

ELSIE CLEWS PARSONS
Interpreter of the Past and Inventor of the Future
34

THE HARVEY GIRLS
The Women Who Tamed the Wild, Wild West
45

MABEL DODGE LUHAN
An Artist of Life
56

FRIEDA LAWRENCE
A Genius for Living
69

MARIA MARTINEZ
Master Potter of San Ildefonso
78

GEORGIA O'KEEFFE
A Woman on Paper
84

LAURA GILPIN
Cowgirl at Heart
94

MILLICENT ROGERS
Collector/Artist of Lifestyle
108

JESUSITA ARAGON
La Partera: Healer and Midwife
115

BIBLIOGRAPHY
126

INDEX
128

ACKNOWLEDGMENTS

Many heartfelt thanks to my editor, Charlene Patterson, for her insight and guidance, and to Josh Rosenberg for his patience and understanding. Thanks also to my mom and dad for introducing me to the special beauty of New Mexico and to Ellen for helping me learn to ride the range. A special wink and a nod to my Hole-in-the-Wall Gang: Pam, John, Mark, Richie, Jason, Nancy, and that adorable Sean, without whom I'd never get away with any of this.

INTRODUCTION

Since the beginnings of civilization, the women of New Mexico have been called upon to provide vast stores of quiet strength, faithful endurance, inspired creativity, and sometimes downright unmitigated gall. In this beautiful but unforgiving "land with lost borders" the women profiled in this book braved battles, saved nations, scaled mountains, and created masterpieces. Through a thousand small but distinct gestures, they helped to make New Mexico a spiritual and cultural mecca for seekers the world over.

The women presented in these pages aren't all that different from us. They faced moments of self-doubt and petty irritations. They fell in love, and not always with the person who was best for them. They had high hopes for their children and worried about things they couldn't change. Yet they somehow managed to let their hearts leap high and through the force of their own personalities were able to change their corner of the world.

I hope that these remarkable women of New Mexico will inspire remarkable readers young and old to transcend the limitations of their lives and discover their own special land of enchantment.

MOTHER MAGDALEN AND THE SISTERS OF LORETTO
1852–1881

Pioneers of Education

*M*other Magdalen stood back and looked with relief and amazement at the miraculous staircase that now joined the main chapel with the choir loft of the chapel of Loretto on the Santa Fe frontier. For twenty years Mother Magdalen and the Sisters of Loretto had lived, worshiped, and educated girls in the small convent area donated to them by Rumaldo Baca. And then finally, in 1873, the Archbishop had agreed that a chapel should be added, and construction of the chapel at Loretto began. Five years later, the Chapel of Loretto, or Our Lady of Light Chapel, was completed, and it was unlike anything that Santa Fe had seen before. The towering altar, ornate statues, stations of the cross, stained-glass windows, and pews had been shipped all the way from Europe to complete the architect's vision of a miniature version of Paris's Sainte-Chapelle cathedral right in the heart of America's southwestern frontier. But of all the remarkable features assembled in this chapel, perhaps the most remarkable is Mother Magdalen's Miracle Staircase.

Interior of the Loretto Chapel, with the miraculous staircase on left

The story of the Sisters of Loretto and their miracle staircase began in 1851 when the Bishop of Santa Fe, John Baptist Lamy, saw a need for the children in his diocese to be educated. An important part of his mission was to build churches and provide education for the people of New Mexico, so he wrote to Archbishop Purcell of Cincinnati and explained his need for six nuns to open a school for girls in his territory:

> I would pay their expenses for coming to this place. . . .
> The Sisters of Notre Dame will receive a letter from me
> . . . I have asked them if they could send me a few
> Sisters to establish a good school . . . or if it was not in
> their power to spare any Sisters, will you please write to
> Emmitsburgh to obtain three or four Sisters of Charity
> . . . or Sisters of any order.

The Sisters of Loretto, who originally called themselves Friends of Mary, were founded in 1812 on the Kentucky frontier. The mission of these original sisters was to educate the poor children of their community. Later, they changed their name to the Sisters of Loretto and began to bring education to the children of other communities, not only throughout the American frontier but also across international borders, into such countries as China, Bolivia, Chile and Peru.

When Bishop Lamy's call for teachers was presented to them, the Sisters of Loretto responded enthusiastically. Mother Matilda and five Sisters resolved to leave their Mother House in Kentucky and head deep into the heart of the southwestern frontier. Santa Fe seemed so remote and strange at this time that only those sisters who had volunteered at some point in their lives for "foreign service" were ordered to go.

After attending mass on June 27, 1852, Mother Matilda and the Sisters began their long and arduous voyage, boarding a steamer bound for St. Louis. In St. Louis they were met by Archbishop Kenrick and spent a few days at the convent in Florissant resting up to gain the strength they would need to face the many miles that lay between the Sisters and their mission in Santa Fe.

From St. Louis Bishop Lamy booked their passage on a steamer to Independence, Missouri, and on July 10, 1852, they set out on the second and most difficult leg of their journey. While aboard the steamer, cholera broke out, which claimed the life of Mother Matilda, the tiny fold's Mother Superior. Once in Independence, the surviving five Sisters had to fight for the right to bury Mother Matilda on Missouri soil, because the fear of cholera was so great at the time that the local people didn't even want the victims of this dreaded disease buried in their vicinity.

Sister Monica, who had also contracted cholera and was seriously ill, couldn't continue the journey. Because of the same local fears, the Sisters had a lot of difficulty finding a place for Sister Monica to rest and recover. Sister Monica was a widow who had converted to the order and had become one of the most devout and beloved members of the fold. Monica was forced to convalesce first in a warehouse and later outside under a tent in the hot summer sun. At last a local family, the Murphys, took pity on the Sisters of Loretto and invited Sister Monica into their home. Due to their kindness and Sister Monica's legendary resilience, she did recover and completed the journey to Santa Fe three years later. Furthermore, her daughter later followed in her mother's determined footsteps and became a Sister of Loretto as well.

Undaunted by loss and sorrow and determined to complete their journey, the four remaining Sisters headed out on August 1,

1852, across the Great Plains in a caravan of covered wagons. Sister Magdalen was appointed Mother Superior in Mother Matilda's place. Unfortunately, however, although they had put the difficulties of the past behind them, their troubles were far from over. After they had covered just a few miles on their great journey westward, the lead wagon threw a wheel, and the axle snapped. To make matters worse, a fierce storm hit, and because of the storm, the sisters had to stay cooped up in the wagons for days, unable to light a fire or prepare hot food as they waited for their lead wagon to be repaired.

At last the sun came out, the repairs were completed, and the journey continued. Just outside of Pawnee Fork, on the sweeping plains of Kansas, they ran into large herds of buffalo and later found themselves surrounded by 300 Indians. The Indians rode round and round the caravan, encircling the frightened Sisters, who had no way of knowing whether the Indians meant them harm or were simply curious hunters drawn by the herds of precious buffalo. Fortunately, the nuns were able to leave Pawnee Fork unharmed. Uncertain of the reception they would receive from other tribes, however, and believing that Indians seldom went on the offensive after sunset, the Sisters continued their journey under cover of darkness.

On September 12, 1852, the Sisters arrived in Cimarron, Kansas, where they were met by Father Joseph Machbeuf. He provided them with fresh animals and clean beds. That night, for the first time in months, the Sisters slept under a roof in clean sheets. They must have been very grateful indeed for these few days of well-deserved and badly needed bed rest before heading out again toward the great unknown.

Finally, on September 26, 1852, Mother Magdalen and the Sisters reached Santa Fe, entering to the exultant welcoming cries of the local inhabitants. Santa Feans crowded the streets, cheering and waving, as the Sisters rode through the welcome arches amidst a pealing of church bells. They entered the Santa Fe cathedral to sing songs of thanks for their safe arrival, accompanied, to their astonishment, by violins and guitars.

Despite their exhilaration over their safe arrival, Mother Magdalen knew that the work had just begun and that the difficulties would be considerable as they faced this new and foreign land. In a letter to her sister, she expressed the depths of her feelings at being transplanted into this strange, new world:

> While I walked alone . . . I was deeply conscious of my utter loneliness in this strange land and of the great distance which separates me from every object which is dear to me in this world. I thought especially of you, my dear sister . . . feelings that caused the silent tears to flow and a low sigh to escape from my heart. But again, as I contemplated the beautiful heavens and thought of our happy home beyond the clouds, I took heart anew to love more and to serve better my good Lord during the days I have yet to pass in this exile.

As was characteristic of Mother Magdalen, however, she wasted little time complaining and set right to work. The Sisters settled in a house at the center of town and immediately began to learn Spanish, as their new students did not speak English. Their home was in the adobe style, which must have seemed strange to these women who were unused to the dirt floors and stretched-muslin windowpanes of the traditional adobes. The same room served as dormitory, study room, and refectory.

And despite the extreme challenges of the time and the territory, the Sisters of Loretto flourished and expanded. One sister even befriended the outlaw known as Billy the Kid, describing him as "a man with qualities to make him great, smothering his best instincts to become a murderer and an outlaw."

Legend holds that because the Sisters of Loretto had cared for one of the Kid's partners for four months while he recovered from a gunshot wound, the Sisters were immune from attacks by outlaws.

The need for more Sisters quickly became evident, and in June of 1855, four more Sisters left the Mother House bound for Mother Magdalen's newly established Academy for Girls, arriving in Santa Fe on July 24. In the meantime a novitiate had been established, and on September 8 of that same year, five young women, all New Mexico natives, were welcomed into the congregation. Mother Magdalen and the other Sisters translated prayers and the rule book of the order into Spanish to accommodate the newest members of their fold.

A fourth group of Sisters made their way from Kentucky to New Mexico to join Mother Magdalen in 1867. On this journey Sister Alphonsa Thompson, an eighteen-year-old Sister of Loretto, died in a skirmish involving local tribes, and she was buried in an unmarked grave on the plains near Cimarron, Kansas. Her companions did not mark her grave because they feared her remains would be desecrated, and though the Sisters returned for her body, no one was ever able to locate her grave again.

In order to accommodate growing numbers of Sisters and students, constant expansion was necessary, and Mother Magdalen was in a perpetual flurry trying to pay off her debts and raise new money to keep her mission to bring education to the children of New Mexico alive and flourishing. In 1869 the Sisters of Loretto established the first school in Las Vegas, moving into a building donated by Rumaldo Baca, a very wealthy and renowned architect who lived in Las Vegas, New Mexico. The design was in the traditional adobe style typical of Baca buildings, with a courtyard at the back and tiny, wooden-framed dormer windows jutting up out of the roof and extending along the second story.

At last the archbishop approved a plan to fund and build a new chapel for Mother Magdalen. Property was purchased, and in 1873 work on the Chapel of Loretto began. Here is how historians describe the chapel's remarkable construction:

> Undoubtedly influenced by the French clergy in Santa Fe, the Gothic Revival–style chapel was patterned after King Louis XVI's private chapel, Sainte-Chapelle in Paris; a striking contrast to the adobe churches already in the area.
>
> Stone for the chapel was quarried from locations around Santa Fe including Cerro Colorado, about 20 miles from Santa Fe near the town of Lamy. The sandstone for the walls and the porous volcanic stone used for the ceiling were hauled to town by wagon.
>
> The ornate stained glass in the Loretto Chapel also made part of its journey to Santa Fe via wagon. Purchased in 1876 from the DuBois Studio in Paris, the glass was first sent from Paris to New Orleans by sailing ship and then by paddleboat to St. Louis, Missouri, where it was taken by covered wagon over the Old Santa Fe Trail to the chapel.

The chapel was completed in 1888, when Mother Magdalen realized that there was no way to access the choir loft, 22 feet above the main level. Carpenters were called in to address the problem, but they all concluded that access to the loft would have to be via ladder since a staircase would take up too much space in the sanctuary of the small chapel.

MOTHER MAGDALEN AND THE SISTERS OF LORETTO

After such a monumental effort to get this chapel constructed, surely Mother Magdalen was not going to be stopped by mere mortal physics or the limitations of state-of-the-art carpentry techniques. And so she and the other Sisters began a nine-day novena to St. Joseph, patron saint of carpenters, and asked him to come to their aid.

Legend says that on the ninth and final day of the novena, a gray-haired man rode up to the convent on the back of a donkey with a chest full of tools tied to his saddle. He asked to speak to Mother Magdalen and offered to build her staircase, but he asked for one thing in return: Mother Magdalen was never to disclose the name of the craftsman.

Mother Magdalen agreed and instructed the Sisters not to speak to the mysterious carpenter and to leave him alone to do his work. Mother Magdalen never divulged her helper's identity, even on her deathbed. Legend holds that the mysterious carpenter went effortlessly about his work and completed the staircase with dispatch. The Sisters who quietly observed the carpenter at work said he used only a saw, a T-square, and a hammer and that he was often observed submerging pieces of wood in large tubs of hot water.

When the carpenter had finished the staircase, Mother Magdalen gathered everyone into the hallway to marvel over this remarkable achievement, but when they turned around to thank their mysterious helper, he had vanished. And what's more, he never sent a bill! After searching for the man (an ad even ran in the local newspaper) and finding no trace of him, stories began to circulate throughout the territory that St. Joseph himself had come to the Loretto Academy to build the miraculous staircase for Mother Magdalen and the stalwart Sisters.

The stairway's carpenter, whoever he was, produced a remarkable staircase. At the time the craftsmanship involved was nothing short of a miracle, and the design considerations still perplex experts. The staircase has two 360-degree turns and no visible means of support. Also, the staircase was built completely without nails. The entire structure is held together with wooden pegs. The hardwood is spliced in seven places on the inside and in nine on the outside. Each piece forms a perfect curve, and no one has ever been able to identify the kind of wood used, although some have suggested that it is some type of exotic hardwood grown in the Middle East. As one climbs the steps, one gets a feeling of vertical lift, as if the staircase were a large, coiled wooden spring. Many people suspect that this springiness is a major part of the creator's secret.

Pilgrims, skeptics, architects, and carpenters all began to visit the Chapel of Loretto to inspect the "miracle staircase," attempting to decipher its mystery. Every lumberyard in New Mexico was approached and questioned, but to this day no one has ever produced even an invoice for the materials the carpenter used.

The miracle staircase was used every day for more than eighty-five years. The Loretto Academy was closed in 1968, and the Chapel of Loretto was informally deconsecrated as a Catholic chapel. Loretto Chapel is now a private museum where people from around the world come to observe the staircase and remember Mother Magdalen and her miraculous mission.

Mother Magdalen, the first Mother Superior of Santa Fe, held her office at the Chapel of Loretto from 1852 to 1881. Her leadership was dynamic. Under her guidance the work of the Sisters was expanded to include schools in Taos in 1863, Mora and St. Mary's Academy in Denver in 1864, Albuquerque in 1866, West Las Vegas in 1869, Las Cruces in 1870, Bernalillo in 1875, and Socorro and San Elizario in 1879. She resigned in 1881 because of poor health and rheumatism, which confined her to her bed for the next thirteen years until her death in 1894.

Many Sisters of Loretto, an order that exists to this day, remain convinced that St. Joseph himself built the miracle staircase, but whatever the origin, there is no question that it is a lasting monument to the strength, flexibility, grace, and endurance of Mother Magdalen and her valiant Sisters, who braved the frontier to bring education and enlightenment to the West. Like Mother Magdalen and the Sisters, its beauty and craftsmanship are ageless, its strength untiring.

NAMPEYO (SNAKE THAT DOES NOT BITE)

1860–1942

Hopi Master Potter

"My daughter, be sure you have your hands. Train your hand so that it feels the pottery. The wall, the thickness of molding, where you are, and especially when you are rubbing your pottery. Make sure your hands are good enough so that you know just how thick your potteries are, where it is thick and where it is thin. And with molding, when you get blind, it is going to show you how you are molding; when you are blind you can still go around it with your feeling. So it won't be too bad, if you can't design. You will be able to just mold it and to rub it. Because you have a feeling of it. You know how the pottery feels."

Nampeyo, which means "snake-that-does-not-bite," is one of the most celebrated Native American potters in the world. She is credited for both the revival of ancient Hopi pottery techniques and the resurgence of contemporary Hopi pottery, but she spent the second half of her creative life blind. She lost her eyesight to trachoma, a disease that was brought to the Southwest by white Europeans. Thus, ironically, the same group of people that brought her worldwide acclaim also brought her blindness.

Nampeyo is given credit for the so-called "Sikyatki Revival," which resurrected the ancient Hopi techniques for fashioning pottery. She was influenced by designs from her own Hopi past but also by cultures other than the Hopi, some ancient and some contemporary. In this sense Nampeyo is credited with the birth of contemporary Hopi pottery, now called Hano Polychrome. Without Nampeyo, Hopi pottery may have remained a lost art, buried in the dust of antiquity.

In order to put Nampeyo's contribution into the proper perspective, it's helpful to understand a little bit about what life was like for the Hopis while Nampeyo was creating her pots. Anglo society had decided that they were going to "civilize" the Hopi and other tribal nations. They began a widespread campaign to Anglicize the Pueblo Indians by imposing white culture upon them, against their will. The goal was to turn all Native Americans into English-speaking, tax-paying Christians, without any understanding of or concern for the Hopi's culture, history, or humanity.

When adults proved too resistant, the campaign turned its attention to the children. Pueblo children over the age of six were kidnapped from tribal lands throughout New Mexico and placed into "Indian Schools," sometimes in states as far away as California. They were forced to cut their hair and wear the white man's clothing, which was a disgrace in Hopi culture. And to make matters worse, the increase in American visitors to Pueblo lands brought diseases such as influenza, smallpox, tuberculosis, and the trachoma that caused Nampeyo's blindness. This decimated Pueblo populations. So Nampeyo's commitment to expressing the ancient techniques and traditions of her Hopi heritage was not only a creative statement but a way to keep the heart and soul of her beleaguered culture alive in an environment that was predisposed to its ultimate destruction.

Nampeyo with some of her pottery

It's also important, when considering the Nampeyo phenomenon, to understand something about the history of Hopi pottery. The heart of Hopi country is located on the tops of three mesas that the European explorers, for the sake of convenience, named First Mesa, Second Mesa, and Third Mesa. Three small villages that still exist occupied the top of First Mesa. The oldest is Walpi on the west, then Sichimovi in the middle, and Hano on the east. The prehistoric Anasazi culture first introduced the art of pottery making to these villages around A.D. 700. The art progressed from a crude gray-ware pinch-pot to more elaborate decorative work around A.D. 1000. The use of colors evolved between the eleventh and the fourteenth centuries.

The fourteenth century was a very important period for ancient Hopi pottery. New clays and firing techniques were discovered, which radically changed the texture of the early pottery, which was originally rough and soft. Suddenly the finish on the pots became much smoother and harder, due to a new kind of slip clay the Hopis had discovered on their land. This resulted in a far superior surface, and elaborate designs painted directly onto the surface of a pot.

Entering the fifteenth century with this new and more refined pottery, the Hopis began experimenting with sophisticated symmetry and design, including the depiction of life forms and stories on the pots. This movement culminated in the development of Sikyatki Polychrome, which was one of the most significant leaps forward in pottery making of that time.

Sityatki Polychrome uses paint made from a mixture of boiled herbs, ground minerals, or colored clays painted directly onto the pot itself. This mixture resulted in more colorful pottery. Now, rather than just black and white and gray pottery, ancient Hopi potters were producing startling palettes of reds, oranges, yellows, and browns. This style lasted until the early 1700s, at which time the quality of Hopi pottery began suddenly to deteriorate. Before long Hopi pottery and thousands of years of design preeminence had all but disappeared, until the emergence of Nampeyo, who revived the ancient Sikyatki artistry of her ancestors.

Nampeyo was of Hopi-Tewa descent. Her birthday is placed at somewhere around 1860. She was born in Hano, a small Hopi-Tewa village on First Mesa. Her mother was a Tewa woman of the Corn Clan from Hano, called White Corn, and her father was a Hopi man from the Snake Clan from nearby Walpi. The Hopi nation is divided into clans such as the Bear Clan, the Snow Clan, and the Snake Clan, and each clan is guided by the attributes of their hallmark, which is rather like a family crest, and the names of clan members usually reflect their clan. Clan affiliation is also reflected in the designs used in each clan's pottery and jewelry. For example, the hallmark of the Snow Clan is a snow cloud, and the hallmark of the Corn Clan is an ear of corn. These clan hallmarks are also found in ancient hieroglyphs marking sacred Hopi territory.

Nampeyo grew up with her mother's Corn Clan family in Hano. She came from a family of potters, so, as was the Hopi way, she became a potter herself, learning the traditional designs and techniques from her mother. Nampeyo was a capable potter and a fully contributing member of her village by the time she was fifteen. By the time Nampeyo was nineteen, she was already a well-recognized potter, and her reputation had reached far beyond the confines of her village.

The Hopis are a deeply religious people, and Nampeyo's early life was filled with the richly textured ceremonies and rituals of Hopi tradition, including colorful kachina dances. Kachina dancers wore masks that represented the spirit guides and retold, in movement, the ancient Hopi legends about creation, hunting, the changing of the seasons, and other fundamental mysteries of life and nature.

So from the beginning Nampeyo's cultural and physical landscapes were colorful, and her entire life was profoundly attached to the contemporary expression of ancient traditions. It's not surprising, therefore, that Nampeyo was drawn to the Hopi and Zuni ruins near her home in Hano. There, with her mother, she made a startling discovery that was to change the course of her life, as well as the creative lives of generations of potters to come after her. She rediscovered the fine slip clay that had allowed her ancient Hopi ancestors to create the unique Sityatki pots. Nampeyo also found artifacts and pottery shards from which she relearned the ancient designs and symmetry and gave them new life in the pottery of contemporary Hopi culture.

Nampeyo was described as a small woman who was kind and gracious. She was also very beautiful, so beautiful, in fact, that her first husband left her because he feared that her beauty would make her an unfaithful wife. In 1878, when Nampeyo was twenty, she married the man who was to become her lifelong husband and creative partner. Lesso was the son of a Walpi elder, and after they married, as is Hopi tradition, Lesso came to live with Nampeyo near her mother's home in Hano. There, they had five children: Annie, 1884; William, 1887; Nellie, 1896; Wesley, 1899; and Fannie, 1900. They were together until Lesso died in 1932, more than fifty years later.

Nampeyo worked on her pots both for use in village life and for sale at the trading post that was opened by Thomas Keam on Hopi land in 1875. Nampeyo lived a quiet life with her family in her village of Hano without much national acclaim until the

1880s, when she began to flower as a nationally recognized artist. As is usually the case, her recognition was the result of a combination of her great skill and a little luck. Public attention had suddenly turned with a great deal of enthusiasm toward the art and culture of the Pueblo Indians during this period. Creatively, philosophically, and spiritually, turn-of-the-century Americans looked to the Southwest for healing truths and a simpler life.

In addition, during the winter of 1888, Richard Wetherill discovered the Cliff Palace and other Anasazi dwellings on Mesa Verde, Colorado. Americans received this discovery with a great deal of hoopla. The national curiosity and preoccupation with the Southwest culminated in the 1892 World's Fair, which featured exhibits showcasing ancient and contemporary southwestern Indian handcrafts, complete with real live Native Americans performing their crafts before the eyes of an amazed public.

While the public spotlight might have been a bit uncomfortable, it did increase the demand for artifacts from the Hopi mesas, including contemporary Hopi pottery, especially pots made by Nampeyo. As a result of this national exposure, the standout quality of Nampeyo's work became the paradigm against which all others were measured.

The new fascination with the Southwest that gripped America also brought many exploratory expeditions to the region. Jesse W. Fewkes, director of the Hemenway Archaeological Expedition, made an expedition to First Mesa in 1891 to explore the abandoned ruins of Sikyatki, the site where Nampeyo collected her shards and learned her craft from the vestiges left by her ancestors. During this first exploratory mission, Fewkes met Nampeyo for the first time.

Fewkes returned in 1895 and spent two months excavating

the Sikyatki ruins. He used local Hopi men to do the excavating and uncovered a vast number of Sikyatki pots, many in remarkably good condition. Some historians say that Nampeyo's husband, Lesso, was employed by the Fewkes expedition and that it was as a consequence of his involvement with this excavation that Nampeyo was led to the shards that inspired her work. Other historians are careful to point out, however, that it is hardly likely that it would take an expedition of white men, new to the region, to point out something on Hopi land to a Hopi. Besides, Nampeyo was already a well-established potter working in the Sikyatki tradition a good ten years prior to Fewkes arrival.

In 1884 the U.S. Army conquered Geronimo and ended once and for all the open warfare with southwestern Indian tribes. Buffalo Bill started his Wild West Show in 1880, and even the great outdoorsman Teddy Roosevelt came west in 1884, which made the Southwest even more popular with American tourists than it already had been. This led to a great literary outpouring about the Southwest in pamphlets, books, and brochures. In addition, socialite Mabel Dodge Luhan had begun attracting to New Mexico a great number of notable artists, who spread the fame of the Southwest worldwide. The 1881 completion of the Santa Fe Railroad through Arizona and the eventual opening of Grand Canyon National Park brought even more activity to Hopi land. Most important for tourism, it brought the Fred Harvey Company.

At the turn of the century, the Southwest was becoming popular as a tourist destination, but getting there was far from the comfortable pleasure trip that would draw the numbers of people that the railroad was hoping for. Accommodations along the railway were scarce, and the food was horrible, making the experience a decidedly less-than-luxurious experience. Trains stopped for only a brief half hour in station towns that were not equipped to handle this new influx of visitors, and often people were left hungry or, worse yet, sick from tainted food that they'd either brought along with them or eaten in haste in a local beanery.

To solve this problem, the Santa Fe Railroad hired a man named Fred Harvey to provide first-class food and lodging to Santa Fe Railroad travelers and to make vacations west a pleasant, rather than a punishing, experience. Fred Harvey delivered fine food in a civilized setting for a reasonable price, all within the half-hour window that train stopovers mandated. He also built large and luxurious "Harvey Houses" all along the Santa Fe line, which snaked its way through the Southwest. Once merely wayhouses where passengers could put up for the evening, these houses eventually became destinations in and of themselves, thanks to the unique charm of Harvey hotels.

Fred Harvey was also a very good businessman and an expert at reading trends. He noticed the new American preoccupation with Native American handcrafts, so he took a tip from the World's Fair and featured Native American art and culture in most of his hotels. With the help of architect Mary Colter, Harvey Houses provided a unique window into Native American culture and featured a generous display of Pueblo Indian arts and crafts, complete with demonstrations of these crafts by the artists themselves. Because of her notoriety, Nampeyo and her family were invited to give demonstrations at Fred Harvey's Hopi House at its opening in 1905. In 1910 the Nampeyo family gave demonstrations at the Chicago Exposition in the Coliseum.

No one is exactly sure when Nampeyo stopped making her unique Sityatki-inspired style of pottery. By 1915 this era had clearly come to a close, and some people believe that her failing eyesight prevented her from carrying on in this highly detailed design style. By 1920 Nampeyo was almost completely blind, and her daughters were painting the designs on most of her pottery. Even Lesso became part of the painting team and was apparently quite talented at it. As Nampeyo's granddaughter tells it: "I learned from Nampeyo, and so did my mother, Annie. Everybody painted for her—Nellie, Fannie and my mother helped her a lot, painted those little fine lines. Her husband, Lesso, he helped, he sure could paint, that old man."

Although many people believed that Nampeyo stopped creating the highly detailed designs of the Sityatki style because her vision declined, Nampeyo's family insists that it wasn't blindness but creative curiosity that inspired Nampeyo to begin experimenting with more tactile and less design-oriented forms.

Nampeyo passed away in 1942, ending an era in Hopi pottery and leaving behind a legacy of craftsmanship and ancient authenticity that prevails to this day. Nampeyo's commitment to resurrecting the ancient techniques of her people was not only a creative vision but one that had a very important social result for the Hopi people and, indeed, all Pueblo Indians. It brought Native American and, in particular, Hopi culture and ancient traditions into Anglo consciousness and forced white society to recognize, for perhaps the first time, the beauty and value of what they were attempting to destroy. In so doing Nampeyo ensured that some aspect of her culture would survive and opened the door to greater understanding and appreciation between Anglo and Native American people.

Neither injustice nor the loss of her eyesight stopped Nampeyo from continuing her craft, nor did it stop her daughters or her granddaughters, who all became potters and many of whom also became blind from the same disease that had taken Nampeyo's vision. But thanks to the skills and innate understanding of the craft, handed down from mother to daughter, the Nampeyo tradition lived on, despite enormous obstacles.

The matriarch of the Nampeyo family would be proud of the fine lineage of potters who have succeeded her, starting with her three daughters—Fannie, Nellie, and Annie—and now extending to her great-grandchildren. The Nampeyo name has become a watermark of excellence in the world of Native American art.

MARY COLTER
1869–1958

Architect of the Earth

The city of St. Paul, Minnesota, grew up on the banks of the Mississippi River, right in the heart of Sioux Indian territory. Because of the prevalence of Indian culture in the region, many homes, including eleven-year-old Mary Jane Colter's, were decorated with Indian art and artifacts. Mary's favorite possession was a collection of Sioux drawings that a friend had given her. Mary was fascinated with the way these simple paintings reflected the land and the culture that had inspired them. They spoke to her of America in a way that the European-inspired landscapes hanging on her parent's walls did not, and she cherished them as her most precious treasure.

In the 1880s a smallpox epidemic swept the Indian community, and Mary's mother burned all of the Indian articles in the house to prevent the spread of disease, except, that is, for Mary's drawings, which Mary hid, preferring to risk smallpox rather than part with them.

Rescuing Indian art and culture from the flame of extinction and putting it on display so that others could appreciate its beauty

Mary Colter at age 23

was an exercise that Mary would repeat again and again, on a much larger scale, for the rest of her life.

Mary Colter's love of ancient cultures and her desire to communicate the beauty she saw guided her long career as an architect and designer for the Fred Harvey Company. Mary succeeded in a "man's job" in a "man's world," opening up a gateway to the West and giving birth to a uniquely American, southwestern style.

Mary Colter was born in Pittsburgh, Pennsylvania, on April 4, 1869. She was the daughter of William and Rebecca Colter, who owned and ran the Hats, Caps and Clothing Store on Butler Street in Pittsburgh. Mary's father grew tired of life in Pittsburgh, however, and moved his family west, hopscotching back and forth from Texas to Colorado and finally to St. Paul in 1880, when Mary was eleven years old.

From the time she was a little girl, Mary Colter was drawn to art. The public schools in St. Paul offered classes in music, drawing, and sculpting to all students. Mary pursued her studies enthusiastically, graduating from high school when she was only fourteen years old. Because of her youth, and perhaps because she was a girl at the turn of the century, Mary was not accepted to any art schools, which relieved her parents who, regardless of how mature and self-directed their daughter was, didn't want her going far away from home at such a tender age.

Mary wasn't able to realize her dream of going to art school until 1886, but her success was marred by a series of unhappy circumstances. Mary's father died of a sudden blood clot in his brain, leaving his wife alone with three unmarried daughters and no visible means of support. Mary convinced her mother to send her to art school so that she could earn money to support the family through teaching, and her mother, at last, agreed.

With money left by her father, Mary attended the California

School of Design in San Francisco, studying art and design. She also worked as an apprentice in an architect's office, which gave her the skills that would serve her later in ways that she probably couldn't have even dreamt of at the time.

Mary graduated in 1890 and returned to St. Paul to find a teaching job to support her mother and sister as she had promised. At the age of twenty-three, Mary settled into a job teaching freehand and mechanical drawing at Mechanic Arts High School in St. Paul. She remained in that position for fifteen years, wondering when her thirst for adventure would finally be satisfied.

Then, one day, quite unexpectedly, everything changed for Mary Colter. While vacationing in San Francisco, she visited a school friend who worked in a Fred Harvey gift shop. Mary told the manager of the shop that she was a designer and was interested in working for the Fred Harvey Company. Although she didn't realize it at the time, Mary's casual comment would change the course of her life.

The Fred Harvey Company worked in tandem with the Santa Fe Railroad, opening luxurious restaurants and hotels along the railway west. The Santa Fe Railroad owned the structures, and, within them, Fred Harvey created a relaxed and comfortable dining and lodging experience that drew an increasing number of travelers to New Mexico, the Grand Canyon, and eventually on to California. Mary's flair for distinctly American architecture and design and her understanding and appreciation of Native American and Spanish cultures made the Fred Harvey Company the perfect arena for Mary to express her vision.

In the summer of 1902, Mary got her chance to prove herself. The Fred Harvey Company wired Mary, offering her a job as the designer and display arranger for the Indian building adjoining their newest property, the Alvarado Hotel in Albuquerque, New Mexico.

Native American arts and crafts had become very popular

Mary Colter at age 50

among tourists. Fred Harvey capitalized on the new public palate for all things Indian by deciding to incorporate a salesroom featuring Indian handicrafts into his new hotel. Mary accepted the job and began what was to become a forty-year relationship with the Fred Harvey Company. In Mary Colter, Fred Harvey had found exactly what he needed to make his new southwestern style a success—an architect with a purely American vision.

Mary went to work with her usual vitality, arranging pots here, piling Navajo blankets there, creating not just a retail display but an entire world that mirrored the ancient culture of the region and plunged patrons into what was for most of them a new and exotic lifestyle.

When the Indian building opened in 1902, Mary returned to her teaching job in St. Paul, but a deep and abiding passion had been ignited in her. She longed for the next opportunity to head west. Finally, in 1904, the Fred Harvey Company called once more and asked Mary to design an Indian building for the El Tovar, a grand hotel they were building on the western rim of the Grand Canyon. This time, Mary would not only be designing the interiors but the very walls themselves. Everything from the ground up would reflect Mary's vision.

Mary Colter's Indian building, called Hopi House, opened on January 1, 1905. Mary's design was guided by a Native American preference for structures that lived in harmony with their natural surroundings and reflected Native American activities and religious beliefs.

One of the Indian rooms in Hopi House housed a Hopi altar, a sand painting, and two religious articles from the deeply spiritual Hopi culture that had never been shared with Anglos before. In addition to the Indian rooms, there was a Spanish-Mexican room and a Totem room, which featured carved masks and bowls fashioned by the northwestern tribes.

With Hopi House Mary Colter created the perfect atmosphere for tourists to rest, relax, and reflect on the beauty of the environment. And then, of course, there was a salesroom so that tourists could take home a souvenir pot or blanket to remind them of their trip. The Hopi House was very popular, and the Fred Harvey Company was becoming increasingly impressed with Mary Colter's style.

After Hopi House was completed, Mary returned to her teaching job in St. Paul, and one can only speculate how anxious she was for the next Fred Harvey project to carry her back to the land and the work that she loved.

In 1908, when an offer from Fred Harvey wasn't yet forthcoming, Mary, hungry for a change, took a job as a display designer and decorator with the Frederick and Nelson Department Store in Seattle, Washington. She moved her entire family from St. Paul to the Pacific Northwest. Sadly, a year later, Mary's mother, Rebecca, developed a dangerous anemia and died on December 17, 1909.

At last, in 1910, fortune smiled, and Mary was offered a permanent position with the Fred Harvey Company. Tourism in the Southwest was booming. Mary was hired to decorate and design all of the new Fred Harvey hotels, restaurants, and facilities. In 1910 it was very unusual for a woman to have such an important and powerful position in a large company. But in addition to competence and vision, Mary also had enough moxie to hold her own managing railroad engineers, contractors, and crews of workmen who weren't used to taking orders from women.

Mary did have a very pronounced personality and a driving work ethic. But she also had an infectious sense of fun, and she knew how to be diplomatic, especially with the Fred Harvey architects who were drawing the working plans for her buildings and with the Fred Harvey Company itself, who was footing the bill.

GRAND CANYON NATIONAL PARK MUSEUM COLLECTION

Hopi House, 1915

Yet, as it is with most dynamic and passionate visionaries, Mary created strong feelings in people. Folks either liked her a lot or not at all, and the reviews from the workmen were varied. Many remembered her as an irritable and difficult taskmaster who scrutinized every detail of construction and rarely compromised. And thanks to an unfortunate tendency to refer to the workmen as her "boys," her crews often referred to Mary as "the old lady." But whether fan or detractor, nobody could argue that Mary had taste and charm. Mary really knew how to make a room look good. Stewart Harvey, Fred Harvey's grandson, said of her, "The charm of the hotels was what she did. She knew how to make something look better than it was."

In 1910 Mary began work on the Fred Harvey Company's

new Kansas City headquarters and the interiors for the new Santa Fe Railway station at Lamy, New Mexico. Lamy was a transfer point just 15 miles south of Santa Fe. The new hotel there, El Ortiz, had been designed by Louis Curtiss in the Mexican adobe style. It was a hacienda-style structure, with the rooms arranged on one level around a courtyard. Mary lavished the interior with expensive, heavy Mexican furniture, Indian pots, and retablos (Spanish religious figures).

When patrons entered the lobby of El Ortiz, Mary wanted them to feel as if they were coming into someone's home as honored guests. After a visit to El Ortiz, Owen Wister, author of *The Virginian*, said, "This little oasis among the desert hills is a wonder taste to be looked back upon by the traveler who has stopped there and forward to by the traveler who is going to stop there. The temptation was to give up all plans and stay a week for the pleasure of living and resting in such a place."

Fred Harvey and Mary Colter turned their gaze back toward the Grand Canyon in 1914. With the arrival of the railroad, tourism had exploded in the region, and the Fred Harvey Company was struggling to keep up with the demand for facilities to accommodate tourists coming to take in the splendor of this natural wonder.

While the Fred Harvey Company considered opting to continue in the Swiss-chalet style that had taken root in the region, they ultimately decided to go with Mary Colter's neoprimitive, southwestern style.

In 1914 Mary worked on Hermit's Rest, an observatory and gift shop built on Hermit Rim Road along the Grand Canyon's edge. The road wound along for 8 breathtaking miles, offering sweeping, epic vistas around every bend, and the drive culminated, at the road's end, with a stop at Mary's triumph of organic architecture.

Visitors enter Hermit's Rest through an arch of seemingly randomly piled rocks, crowned with a broken mission bell. The actual building looks like a pile of haphazardly arranged stone and timber, with a chimney rising like a primitive steeple from the low crouch of the hideaway. It is a remarkable structure, seemingly springing out of the earth. Seen from a distance, the building virtually becomes one with the canyon's face. Upon the building's completion, visitors from far and wide agreed it was the most imaginative rest stop they had ever seen.

Hermit's Rest contained a fireplace alcove and a salesroom where postcards, photographs, and paintings were sold. But the most valuable thing that Hermit's Rest offered was free for the taking: a spectacular view of the Grand Canyon, stunningly framed by Mary Colter's sensitive and imaginative eye.

In 1921 a 420-foot-long swinging suspension bridge stretching across the Colorado River was completed, making the inner canyon accessible to travelers. Mary Colter then began work on the Fred Harvey Company's newest venture, Phantom Ranch. Phantom Ranch is a community of cabins and a large hall, arranged in a cluster at the end of the mule trail at the very bottom of the canyon. When the ranch opened, Mary Colter, at the age of fifty-three, and her sister Harriet, fifty-nine, took the mule trip to the bottom of the canyon for the opening celebration.

Next, Mary and the Fred Harvey Company turned their attention to New Mexico once more, with the renovation of the Alvarado Hotel in Albuquerque. The Alvarado had developed a reputation for some of the region's best celebrity sightings. And as had become characteristic of the Fred Harvey Company, they noticed a popular trend and capitalized on it. They began renovations on the hotel, doubling its capacity and making it the largest Fred Harvey hotel in the world. The Alvarado Hotel, with its aura of glamour and celebrity, was designed to play to the growing California mystique. It invited travelers westward, toward the land of movie stars and orange groves.

From 1923 to 1946 Mary Colter created many new buildings and interiors for the Fred Harvey Company including El Navajo in Gallup, New Mexico; La Fonda in Santa Fe; and the Bright Angel Lodge at the Grand Canyon. Mary Colter retired in 1946 and moved into her new home on the Plaza Chamisal in Santa Fe. She lived to see her work celebrated as some of the most unique and creative American design visions, but she also lived long enough to see many of her beloved buildings go on the auction block.

For Mary Colter it was a tragedy watching her buildings be dismantled and sold. Mary observed, "There's such a thing as living too long."

Mary Colter worked as an architect and a designer for forty years, creating environments that revealed the beauty of the American West for generations of tourists the world over. Mary Colter's structures and interiors introduced a new and truly American spirit to architecture and design, turning away from European-inspired stylization toward a uniquely American simplicity and an organic harmony with the land.

When American tourists turned away from rail travel, many of Mary Colter's buildings were torn down, but many of her buildings, such as Hermit's Rest and the Bright Angel Lodge, remain. They are a testament to Mary's comfortable and sensitive appreciation for the beauty of American cultural diversity, which is at the heart of New Mexican and American life.

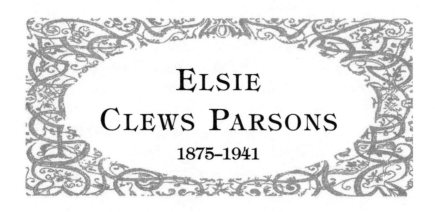

ELSIE CLEWS PARSONS
1875-1941

Interpreter of the Past and Inventor of the Future

$\mathcal{E}$lsie and her colleague made their way in a buggy over the desolate New Mexican countryside toward Hopi territory. Their mission was to witness a Hopi ceremony and begin to gather first-hand data to compile an accurate anthropological study of Pueblo culture. It was Elsie's hope that her unique view of the Pueblos would enlighten white society, teaching them that Native American culture was not dead but alive and constantly evolving. As they made their way toward the mesa, Elsie hoped that this time things would turn out differently.

The year before Elsie Parsons and her colleague from the American Museum of Natural History, preeminent anthropologist Franz Boas, had endured a difficult journey to visit the Zunis in Laguna, only to be turned away in the final moment and excluded from the ceremonial proceedings. As Elsie herself put it in a letter to her husband, Herbert:

18 hours in a buggy the first day, the second, training and motoring to Zuni and up most all night watching a ceremonial from outside a window. . . . the windows of the house across the way were left open and from our terrace we could hear the singing of the cheani (priests). . . . For an hour or so we sat listening to the singing and looking at the dark figures that now and then passed under the terrace, then the Professor (Boas) betook himself to his paradym [sic] of baffling verbs and I in no agreeable state of mind went to bed.

Now, a year later, in 1920, Elsie and Franz Boas were once again on their way to a Pueblo ceremony, and Elsie hoped that the Hopis would be more welcoming than the Zunis had been. Elsie had reasons to be hopeful as they approached Hopi land at the base of the First Mesa. For one thing the western Pueblos were reputed to be more tolerant of Anglo intervention. And Elsie was a little better prepared after the hard-won lessons at Zuni. Elsie carried a photograph, given to her by Flora Zuni, of Flora's Hopi friend George Cochisi. Elsie carried it as a "letter of reference" that she hoped would help her gain access to the pueblo. Flora had given Elsie the photograph knowing, as Elsie said later, "how reassuring to any Pueblo Indian on meeting a stranger is the knowledge of having a common friend."

When they arrived on Hopi land, Elsie checked in at the post office/store as was the custom, and found George Cochisi's aunt. This woman took Elsie and Franz up to the mesa-top town of Sichumovi, in the heart of Hopi country.

Just as Flora and Elsie had hoped, when he saw his picture, George Cochisi gave Elsie and Franz a friendly reception and offered them a room. Elsie was initially concerned that this pueblo had been hopelessly contaminated by Anglo culture when she was

Elsie Clews Parsons

told that only a few short weeks before Douglas Fairbanks had stayed in the same room she was being given. But on a preliminary stroll through the neighboring village of Walpi, she was comforted to discover Indian prayer sticks, a shrine, and other traditional Hopi ceremonial objects. Here at last, she must have thought to herself, was a thriving Pueblo culture that she could experience and interpret. While there was certainly evidence of Spanish and American intervention in her accommodations, it was, she said later, "the old story, as old as Spanish occupation, of foreign goods and contrivances fitted into native concepts and habits of mind."

Elsie's visit with the Hopis exceeded even her most optimistic expectations. On the morning of the winter-solstice ceremony, Elsie had her hair ceremonially washed with yucca suds and her face rubbed with cornmeal in a ritual that was meant to cleanse her of her old name and her old history and allow her to start anew. To Elsie, who had rebelled against social traditions from her earliest days, this must have been a very invigorating experience indeed. That evening, during the ceremony, a Hopi man called Sihtaimi made the unprecedented gesture of making Elsie an adopted member of his family to discourage those members of the tribe who might criticize him for allowing a white person to attend their sacred service.

After the ceremony Elsie, in a letter to her husband, Herbert, described her remarkable time with the Hopis in this way: "So my fund of knowledge of Pueblo Indians is materially increased and coordinated in many particulars. My own rite consisted of being taken into the community through baptism—head washing and name giving—and the acquiring of a father and a large number of aunts, Affly Yu yu hunoma or cloud-covering-falling-rain."

This remarkable introduction into the world of Pueblo culture set the course for Elsie and Boas's next three years of study. They spent their time exhaustively surveying southwestern pueblos. Boas, a language expert, focused on documenting language and collected myths and folktales. Elsie focused on ceremony, social organization, acculturation, and Pueblo psychology.

Elsie's investigation culminated in the massive two volumes of *Pueblo Indian Religion*, originally published in 1939. Franz Boas described the volumes as containing "a summary of practically all we know about Pueblo religion and an indispensable source book for every student of Indian life." But as her life exemplifies, Elsie Clews Parsons's interpretations of culture did much more than educate the public about Indian life. They offered a new way to interpret our own culture. At its core her philosophy sought to set individuals free from restrictive social mores, which she herself had begun rebelling against from a very early age. In this sense Elsie's journey to New Mexico's pueblos began a long time before she actually arrived, back in the heart of New York City.

The combination of self-confidence, courage, intelligence, and irreverence that characterized Elsie's later years were evident from the time Elsie was just a little girl. Elsie Clews was born on November 27, 1875, in New York City, although Elsie, always anxious to disconnect from the past, claimed not to remember when or where she was born, or even how old she was. On her fiftieth birthday her husband, Herbert Parsons, consulted Elsie's mother's family Bible and informed Elsie of the exact time and location of her birth and, thus, of her age.

Elsie was the eldest of three children and the only daughter of Henry Clews, the son of a Staffordshire potter who had immigrated to the United States and founded a New York bank. Elsie's mother, Lucy Madison Worthington, was a descendant of President James Madison and had enjoyed great social prominence for a time. Unfortunately, the Worthington family had fallen into disfavor as a consequence of a scandal involving her mother's notoriously beautiful sister, a Washington hostess called Aunt "Puss." Puss's husband, General William Belknap, was accused of malfeasance while in office, and Puss, in an attempt to shield her husband, took the blame upon herself. The result was a great social outcry against Washington's former sweetheart, the taint of which radiated out into her entire family.

So from the beginning Elsie grew up in an environment that intensely felt the pressure of social restrictions. And it was perhaps this air of scandal that established Elsie's tendency to run full throttle in defiance of social norms and to study the anthropological origins of social custom in order to eradicate those customs that restricted the full and creative expression of individuality. The distinguished Berkeley anthropologist Alfred Kroeber described the beginnings of Elsie's career in this way: "Her society had encroached on her. She studied the science of society the better to fight back against society."

As a young girl Elsie was athletic and sociable, and she often set her mother on edge by refusing to do the kinds of things that New York society girls were supposed to do. She played in the park with boys, eschewed white lace and party gloves, and preferred to stay in her room reading rather than put on stays and go visiting with her mother. Even more alarming to her mother, Elsie refused to be a debutante, preferring instead to pursue a college education and, even worse yet, to specialize in fields that were traditionally dominated by men.

And then, at last, love visited Elsie for the first time and threatened to overthrow all of her unconventional notions and lead her into a more traditional lifestyle. Sam Dexter was a broad, handsome, athletic young man Elsie met in 1893 while summering in Newport. They shared a passionate intellectual attachment as well as being sexually compatible. In addition, they shared a love of athletics.

Talk of marriage was in the air, and Lucy Clews, Elsie's mother, was thrilled to see her daughter falling in love at last, as she had always believed that only love would topple the headstrong Elsie's willfulness and bring her into conformity with the world of proper wives and mothers. Fate, however, had a different destiny in mind for Elsie, and sadly, for Sam as well. In May of 1894 Sam Dexter died of a sudden illness, and for a time, Elsie's heart was completely shattered. His death, however, propelled Elsie on a new course right into the heart of her own destiny as a leading public intellectual of her time and a philosophical mother of the modern age.

To cope with the loss of Sam, Elsie dedicated herself even more passionately to her intellectual pursuits. She entered college, graduating from the newly founded Barnard College in 1896. She went on to receive her master's degree from Columbia in 1897 and a Ph.D. in 1899 in sociology. Her doctoral dissertation, *The Educational Legislation and Administration of the Colonies*, was published as her first book.

In 1895 Elsie had just begun to immerse herself in solving New York's social problems when she met Herbert Parsons, a New York attorney and politician. Herbert fell head-over-heels in love with Elsie, and while Elsie returned Herbert's affections, she had taken a firm stand against marriage, believing that when a woman married, her professional concerns and autonomy vanished. For two years Herbert worked to convince Elsie that marriage would not squelch her independence or her "new womanhood," and, at last, in 1900, Elsie and Herbert Parsons were married and began what became for Elsie an experiment in a new and less-restrictive model for modern marriage.

Though married and later the mother of four children, Elsie

turned her seemingly limitless reserves of energy and wealth to furthering her causes of pacifism, feminism, and anthropology. Her work took her frequently away from her husband, who consoled himself with an extramarital affair. Overcoming her jealousy, Elsie herself engaged in a series of affairs with such men as architect Grant LaFarge and author Robert Herrick. Herbert and Elsie, however alternative their views on marriage, remained together until the end of their lives.

Elsie taught sociology at Barnard as a Hartley House Fellow from 1899 to 1902 and as a lecturer from 1902 to 1905. In 1919 she taught at the opening session of the New School for Social Research, which she had helped found. In addition, Elsie served as a mentor and patron for dozens of young anthropologists. Finally, she dedicated a great deal of her time and energy to writing and research.

Elsie published *The Family* (1906), *Religious Chastity* (1913, published under the pseudonym John Main to protect her husband's political career), *The Old Fashioned Woman* (1913), *Fear and Conventionality* (1914), *Social Freedom* (1915), and *Social Rule* (1916).

Despite the considerable attention these books received in the press for their unorthodox views on femininity, sexuality, love, and marriage, they did not sell well. Nevertheless, Elsie remained committed to discussing the interrelations between individuals and the cultures in which they live and looked for new ways to express her views to a wider audience.

Though these early sociological works, unlike her later anthropological writings, are not recognized as having made a permanent contribution to science, many celebrated intellectuals, including H. L. Mencken, applauded their merits: "I know of no other work," he said, "which offers a better array of observations upon that powerful complex of assumptions, prejudices, instinctive reactions, racial emotions and unbreakable vices of mind which enters so massively into the daily thinking of all of us."

The second stage of her anthropological career began when Elsie was about forty years old. She came to recognize that generalized psychological and philosophical arguments were not making her case strongly enough, and she took her work into the field to view cultures from an anthropological and a historical perspective. The rest of her life was devoted to the fieldwork she loved and that she believed would ultimately illuminate her own society as well as the other cultures she so meticulously investigated.

It was during this time that Elsie studied the pueblos of New Mexico, and the commingling of ancient tradition and foreign intervention she experienced there became central to Elsie's philosophy of active, evolving culture. This philosophy of a constantly mutating cultural identity radiated far beyond just an analysis of the southwestern pueblos. As Desley Deacon explains it in her biography of Elsie Clews Parsons, *Inventing a Modern Life:*

> Elsie Clews Parsons was a "carrier of culture rather than its freight." Born in 1874 in the wake of the American Civil War, she helped create modernism— a new way of thinking about the world that has given the twentieth century its distinctive character. . . . Elsie Clews Parsons—feminist, anthropologist, public intellectual—was a leader in this revolution, using the new cultural anthropology to "kill" nineteenth-century ideas of classification and hierarchy, and to establish new twentieth-century standards of sexual plasticity and cultural tolerance. In a new world that stressed secularism, empiricism, honesty, pluralism in thought and social relationships, and a fluid, constantly evolving self, the "new woman" was, in Parsons' words, "the woman not yet classified, perhaps not classifiable." And a vital

culture was one that could, like the southwestern Pueblos she studied, "keep definite cultural patterns in mobile combination."

Elsie never abandoned the moral ideals and social experiments she so passionately put forth in her early books. Elsie remained a resolute iconoclast until the end of her life, but she became less concerned with public outcry, realizing that in the long run, her exhaustive and meticulously compiled scientific work would convince future generations of the legitimacy of her position.

Elsie received many accolades from her colleagues while she lived. She was president of the American Folklore Society from 1919 to 1920 and served as associate editor of its journal from 1918 until her death. She served as treasurer from 1916 to 1922 and president of the American Ethnological Society from 1923 to 1925. Most significantly, in 1940 she was the first woman elected president of the American Anthropologist Association.

As Deacon puts it, Elsie Clews Parsons pioneered "a new, flexible morality based on sincerity and privacy," evident in her desire to enable women and men to enjoy "trial marriage, divorce by mutual consent, access to reliable contraception, independence and elasticity within relationships, and an increased emphasis on obligations to children rather than to sexual partners."

Elsie's anthropological fieldwork in the American Southwest changed the way that Americans thought about the Pueblos and the way anthropologists conducted field studies as a whole. Deacon claims that Parsons "blazed the trail for almost all of the new developments in the discipline: acculturation studies, biography and autobiography, ethnohistory, community studies, and applied anthropology."

Elsie Clews Parsons died on December 18, 1941, from kidney failure following an emergency appendectomy. True to form, she left the following iconoclastic and unorthodox instructions for the disposal of her remains:

"Directions after death: If convenient, cremation, otherwise, if not convenient, burial, but not in a cemetery and without grave stone. No funeral, and no religious services whatsoever. Relatives requested not to wear mourning."

Elsie managed to ignore boundaries and circumvent ceremony even in death. Her instructions were carried out to the letter. Her son said later, "She wasn't buried anywhere, and there is no headstone."

Elsie Clews Parsons was a relentlessly modern woman, a trailblazing feminist, a respected and innovative anthropologist, a passionate crusader for social causes, and a provocateur who dared Americans to rethink their most fundamental social structures and become more tolerant of individuality.

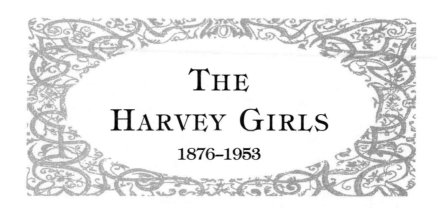

THE HARVEY GIRLS
1876–1953

The Women Who Tamed the Wild, Wild West

Wanted, young women of good character, attractive and intelligent, 18 to 30, as waitresses in Harvey Eating Houses on the Santa Fe Railroad in the West. Wages $17.50 per month with room and board. Liberal tips customary. Experience not necessary.

Advertisement appearing in East Coast newspapers, 1889

While the West may have been won with rifles, spurs, and swinging saloon doors, the Harvey Girls taught the wild, wild West how to mind its manners.

In the late 1800s, when conventional wisdom decreed that women who worked were socially inferior and morally suspect, an English gentleman named Fred Harvey brought thousands of young women west to do respectable work in restaurants along the Santa Fe Railroad line.

The well-scrubbed and crisply dressed "young women of good character" that Fred Harvey trained and installed in his

Harvey Girls

restaurants in New Mexico and other points of interest along the Santa Fe line brought refinement, grace, and stability to the still largely untamed American frontier. But why did these well-brought-up young ladies choose to leave the comfort and civility of their homes in the East and travel to the outposts of civilization populated with unwashed cowboys, gunslingers, and a startling lack of sanitation? For the same reason men went—to seek their fortune.

In the nineteenth century young women didn't have a lot of opportunities for adventure and excitement. Women were expected to stick to home, hearth, and family. Seeking one's fortune in the West was something primarily reserved for men. If women did go to work, it was generally as schoolteachers, clerks, factory workers, or servants—not the most exciting fare for a young woman with big dreams and a bad case of wanderlust. So when Fred Harvey's ad appeared in Eastern newspapers asking for waitresses to come work along the Santa Fe line, women came in droves to apply for their "ticket to ride." Becoming a Harvey Girl gave a woman a chance to leave her past behind and begin a new life.

Many of the Harvey Girls were farmers' daughters who hadn't married and were trying to help their struggling families by working outside the home. Opal Sells was a farmer's daughter who was caring for her invalid mother when she might have been spending her time finding a husband. When her mother died, Opal went to business school to learn to be a secretary. But her boss thought that one of Opal's duties included sitting on his lap. So when Opal saw the Fred Harvey advertisement in the paper, she went straight away, armed with determination and her native spunk, and landed a job as a Harvey Girl. Opal remembers her first day on the job this way:

He (the manager) said to me, "You're the first girl today who wasn't chewing gum. You look like our type." He hired me the next day and I began work the next morning. I was real nervous. They had such a reputation. You started out right from the beginning. No nail polish, no gum, skirts a certain length from the floor and obeying the rules in the dormitory. People said it was degrading work in a restaurant. This was not so at Fred Harvey's.

Other Harvey Girls were college students. Fred Harvey would arrange their schedules so that they could attend classes during their time off from work, and their managers would oversee their grades to make sure that the girls were living up to their potential and attending to their studies. Juddi Morris, author of *The Harvey Girls: The Women Who Civilized the West*, recounted the story of the Meyers sisters:

The two Meyers sisters grew up on a ranch their father homesteaded not far from Las Vegas, New Mexico. Alice and Bernice knew they could go to college only by working, so they took jobs at the Castaneda Harvey House in 1932. The manager liked them, was impressed that they were determined to go to school, and gave them part-time jobs. . . . Alice says that at first, "because of my age—16 or 17—Mr. Lindsay, the manager, questioned my working there, but he reconsidered when he found out I only wanted part-time work and would be attending college. He was listed as my guardian, and my grades were sent to him." During vacation, the sisters worked at special dinners, banquets, and events at Harvey Houses in larger towns up and down the line. Tips at those functions were big, and Bernice remembers that one night she made thirty-one dollars, which paid for her books for a semester.

The "Harvey Way," in which all the Harvey Girls were trained, stressed discipline, cleanliness, and quality. This reassured young women and their families that in Fred Harvey's care, they would be well taken care of. And Fred Harvey did not betray their confidence in him.

The managers of the Harvey restaurants (and sometimes the managers' wives) closely supervised Harvey Girls. The girls lived in carefully controlled dormitories where curfews were strictly enforced. Men were not welcome. Harvey Girls were not allowed to wear jewelry or rouge, and they had to keep their clothing spotless at all times. This was not all that difficult for them, as their laundry was done for them in Albuquerque and shipped out daily via the Santa Fe Railroad to the Harvey Houses all along the line.

Harvey Girls were taught proper manners and behavior and were expected to follow instructions without question. White uniforms were to be worn for breakfast and lunch, whereas black uniforms with white aprons were reserved for the more formal dinner hours. Waitresses worked from morning until night, seven days a week, in shifts that were often split to accommodate train arrivals and departures. For her efforts each girl was given a room and board, $30 a month plus tips, and a free rail pass that would take her anywhere the Santa Fe Railroad went.

"The Harvey Girls were from families that needed the money," Maxine Edwards, Director of the Harvey Girl Museum, said. "Most were from rural areas." Harvey had strict standards, and the Harvey Girls came to believe that they were a cut above the average waitress. "If you were trained as a Harvey Girl," Edwards explained, "you could get a job anywhere."

Fred Harvey's strict codes of conduct applied not only to his waitresses but to every single detail of his fine dining establishments. This insistence upon quality and consistency made Fred Harvey one of the most successful restaurateurs of his day.

Fred Harvey was born in London in 1835 and immigrated to the United States at the age of fifteen. He opened his first restaurant in St. Louis at the age of nineteen. The Civil War put Fred Harvey's restaurant out of business, and he went to work as mobile mail clerk on the Hannibal and St. Joe Railroad. Thus the marriage of restaurants and railroads was stirred in Fred Harvey's mind, or rather, in his stomach.

While working for the railroad, Fred Harvey developed a chronic bellyache, which may have been an ulcer, caused no doubt by too much bad railroad food. And Fred Harvey wasn't alone. In those days, almost without exception, food on the rails was horrendous. The railroad companies did not offer meal service, leaving passengers to fend for themselves in a culinary wasteland. Trains stopped in the stations for approximately twenty minutes, and passengers had to scramble through the frontier dust to locate the nearest eatery. There they would wolf down some unpalatable and, no doubt, unsanitary meal before rushing back to the station. Juddi Morris describes it this way in *The Harvey Girls*:

> Hungry travelers, pressed for time and fearful of being left behind, bolted from the train and stampeded like a herd of buffalo into the small roadside lunch stands. As Keith L. Bryant, Jr. tells it, "there they grabbed greasy doughnuts and lukewarm, bitter coffee (made once a week); rancid bacon; heavy, cold biscuits called sinkers; bowls of gray stew full of strange looking objects (they hoped were vegetables); antelope steak so tough you couldn't get your fork into the gravy; and worst of all,

the dreaded and notorious railroad pie; two crusts as tasteless as cardboard, held together by a glue of suspicious looking meat and shriveled potatoes." Cooks who had been trained in mining or logging camps and had been fired because of inedible cooking often prepared this food. Service was sloppy, and the surroundings and waitresses were filthy. Passengers elbowed and shoved one another to get served, and then bolted down the awful stuff anywhere they could grab a seat or find a place to stand. Fistfights were often the deciding factor in who would get a chair at the counter.

Obviously, if railroad tourism was ever going to thrive as an industry, something was going to have to be done about the food situation. And Fred Harvey, fueled by instinct and indigestion, thought that he was just the man to do it. Fred Harvey proposed to the railroads that he open restaurants in their stations, offering good food and good service at a reasonable price—and all within twenty minutes! Other railroads turned him down, but the Santa Fe saw the wisdom of Fred Harvey's plan. The Santa Fe agreed to provide the restaurant sites and free transportation for Harvey's supplies. Harvey would supply his soon-to-be-legendary good food and fine service. He opened his first restaurant for the Santa Fe in 1876, and it was an instant success. More restaurants followed. Tourism in the American Southwest became enormously popular now that train passengers could look forward to a Fred Harvey meal.

Fred Harvey's success was, of course, based first and foremost on the fine food he served to tourists who were used to putting up with far cruder fare. Harvey served large portions that were always consistent, no matter where along the Santa Fe line a passenger might find himself or herself. It is said that his last words to his son before dying were, "Don't slice the ham too thin."

Fred Harvey food was always served on fine china. The tea or coffee was poured from polished silver pots by gracious and impeccably groomed Harvey Girls who had been well trained in the fine art of hospitality.

So, as important as the generous and delicious, but still reasonably priced, food was to the Harvey system, it was the elegant service provided by the celebrated Harvey Girls that put the icing on the cake and taught the wild and woolly West the meaning of refinement.

By 1880 railroad tourism in the Southwest was booming, and many women came to New Mexico to work in Harvey Houses across the state. Harvey Girls were young, pretty, and refined, uncustomary for women in New Mexico at the time. And the hope of catching the eye of one of the Harvey Girls no doubt kept many a poor New Mexican farmer, rancher, or railroader coming back again and again, not just for the meal, but for the pretty, gentle maiden who served it to him. As the mystique of the Harvey Girls grew, a songwriter of the era, S. E. Kiser, penned a verse in their honor:

> Oh, the pretty Harvey Girl beside my chair,
> A fairer maiden I shall never see,
> She was winsome, she was neat,
> She was gloriously sweet,
> And she certainly was very good to me.

Will Rogers was reported to have added that "Fred Harvey kept the West in food and wives."

So in addition to offering women new professional and regional horizons and a good living, working for Fred Harvey also became known as a surefire way to get a husband during a time when women outnumbered men in the East five to one. It has been estimated that about 4,000 babies born to former Harvey Girls were named Fred or Harvey.

La Fonda, in Santa Fe, New Mexico, was one of the premier Harvey Houses along the Santa Fe line. Architect Mary Colter designed the building in 1922, but it was built on the site of previous inns dating back to Santa Fe's founding in 1602. In 1821, when Captain William Becknell completed the first successful trading expedition from Missouri to Santa Fe—a route that came to be known as the Santa Fe Trail—he enjoyed the hospitality of the La Fonda Inn where the Santa Fe Trail terminated at the town's central plaza.

Only the most senior Harvey Girls warranted a coveted slot at La Fonda. For this reason La Fonda's experienced and celebrated staff trained many new Harvey Girls.

Harvey Girls, if accepted for employment, boarded a Santa Fe train and headed west to begin their rigorous training. They were often sent to New Mexico, usually to La Fonda, for a period of training that was often described to be as difficult as boot camp.

The train trip to "boot camp" was paid for by the railroad, and Harvey Girls traveled first class. All along the way, trainees ate in Harvey Houses, and when they finally reached their destination, they were fitted for uniforms and put on duty full-time, assigned to follow, observe, and assist more experienced Harvey Girls. The training period lasted thirty days, and pay did not start until training was finished.

At La Fonda, as in other Harvey Houses, the menu was fixed, and the price was 75 cents per person. For drinks each diner had a choice of coffee, tea, and milk or iced tea. The beverage choice was relayed to the drink server by the position of the cup and saucer in front of each patron. Train passengers had only twenty

ARIZONA STATE LIBRARY, ARCHIVES AND PUBLIC RECORDS

Harvey House Staff, circa 1920

minutes at each train stop, and this made efficiency by the staff extremely important.

When Harvey Girls weren't serving the passengers from a waiting train, they would make sandwiches, slice pies (five slices per pie, not six) or make soups and salad dressings. Harvey House staffs were often large. In addition to the fifteen to thirty Harvey Girls, there could also be butchers, bakers, busboys, pantry girls, housemaids, managers, and other staff.

Many Harvey Girls worked for the Fred Harvey Company for decades. Others left the company but stayed on in the Southwest, often marrying ranchers, miners, or railroad men.

Many became founding members of the small communities that sprang up along the rails.

These women and the Santa Fe Railroad served as links between America and its expanding frontier. As Lenore Dill, who worked for the Santa Fe Railroad, put it, "Many children and grandchildren of former Harvey Girls could boast about their mother or grandmother being a true pioneer, and coming west with the Harvey Houses. It carries a great deal more prestige than coming west in a covered wagon, but only a lady could become a Harvey Girl."

To the frontier outposts of the West, once places where one could encounter stampeding buffalo herds, Indian attacks, train robbers, and horse thieves, the Harvey Girls brought culture, refinement, civility, and romance, thus opening up the West for us all.

MABEL DODGE LUHAN
1879–1962

An Artist of Life

*I*n April of 1919, weary, confused, and badly in need of a renewed sense of purpose, Mabel Dodge Luhan went to visit Mrs. Dudley, a popular fortuneteller in New York City.

Mabel leaned across the table and looked deeply into Mrs. Dudley's eyes, trying to divine where her long and winding path might lead her. Mrs. Lorus Dudley gazed into her crystal ball and seemed to find the answers for which Mabel was looking. She told Mabel that Taos, New Mexico, was "the beating heart of the world". She explained that "great souls" would be drawn there and that Mabel had been chosen to be the bridge between the Indian and Anglo people. Only then, she emphasized to Mabel, would people find the psychic key to nirvana on earth.

Mabel left Mrs. Dudley's parlor elated. She made plans to return to Taos immediately. Just a short time ago she had left New Mexico frustrated and confused, and now here she was returning with a whole new sense of certainty and commitment.

Mabel believed that she had been singled out for a great purpose—to be a bridge between cultures, to wed European and

Native American philosophies, and to heal the ailing, postwar American soul.

Mabel's ability to infuse the world with her bright and unusual vitality didn't descend, fully crafted, out of the blue. Mabel had spent a lifetime rebelling against the oppressive and unfeeling conventions of wealthy, Victorian society. And she had a long history of inviting the latest and the greatest celebrities to her home hearth and converting them to her passionate, messianic vision of life as art.

Mabel's passion for beauty, art, and the life of the imagination was grounded in a lonely and unorthodox history. She was born in Buffalo, New York, in 1879. As the only child of a wealthy New York family, Mabel suffered from a form of upper-class child abuse. She lived with two parents from affluent families who lived off their inherited wealth, showing little interest in life and little love for each other or their children. Mabel said she couldn't remember ever being touched, loved, hugged, or even scolded. She had every kind of support that money could buy, but she lived in an emotional vacuum; in some respects she spent the rest of her life trying to find a way to fill that void.

Mabel studied briefly in New York City and at a finishing school near Washington, D.C., before entering Buffalo society in 1897. In her first calculated act of social rebellion, she bobbed her hair and married Karl Evans, a handsome but completely heedless young man of her class, in 1900. Her father was furious, and Mabel was thrilled to have at last had some kind of an emotional impact on her distant father, even if it was invoking outrage. But her new role as a society wife soon lost its appeal. The marriage turned out to be short-lived, however, as her young husband was accidentally shot and killed while hunting just a few months after the birth of their son, John.

Mabel Dodge Luhan

Karl's death, combined with the unexpected death of her father a few months before, threw the already unstable Mabel into a deep depression, and she made a halfhearted attempt at suicide. Her family sent Mabel and her young son to Europe to recover. During the voyage Mabel met Edwin Dodge, an architect from Boston who pursued her passionately. Mabel and Edwin married in Paris in 1905 and moved to Florence, Italy, where Mabel began work on the first of many palaces of the heart that she would construct in her lifetime

The Villa Curaria had been built on the hilltops above Florence for the Medici during the Renaissance. Mabel's restoration of the villa occupied the next few years of her life, as she transformed its cavernous halls and drafty chambers into a lavish mirror of her internal landscape. Each room in the house was designed in a different period, to represent Mabel's mercurial moods. The house became a sweeping canvas for Mabel to express her artistic vision of herself.

When the house was complete, Mabel used herself as a canvas. She transformed herself into a Renaissance hostess and dressed in the clothes of the period. She gave extravagant dinner parties that were attended by the great actors and writers of her day. Pianist Arthur Rubinstein performed at the villa, and Gertrude Stein visited often, as did Alice B. Toklas and Eleanore Duse, to name just a few.

In her heart of hearts, Mabel believed that she was giving birth to a new Renaissance. It soon became clear, however, that while Mabel had created a glorious frame, the picture itself was missing. By 1912, more nervous and erratic than ever, and with her second marriage failing, Mabel returned to New York with Edwin and John Evans.

Mabel and Edwin's attempt to save their marriage by returning to New York proved disastrously ineffective. In their home on Twenty-fifth Street and Fifth Avenue, Mabel grew even more depressed and ultimately convinced a doctor that Edwin's emotional inaccessibility was at the heart of her unhappiness. The doctor advised Edwin to move out in the interests of his wife's health, and Edwin, exasperated, at last consented to find his own apartment. Relieved of the burden of a loveless marriage, Mabel began transforming herself into her next persona—a radical, avant-garde New York hostess.

Mabel's new salon on the edge of Greenwich Village became a celebrated gathering place for a new stream of artists and social activists who were opposed to the inhumane, Industrial Age philosophies that governed American social practice at the beginning of the twentieth century. Mabel supported both the famous Armory Show of 1913 and the Paterson Strike Pageant, an extravaganza held at Madison Square Garden to support striking textile workers in New Jersey. Mabel spoke out for everything that was modern, from Gertrude Stein's prose to Freud's psychology to Margaret Sanger's birth-control clinic, and came to be known as the quintessential embodiment of the modern woman.

During this period Mabel had an intense affair with the revolutionary journalist John Reed. The tempestuous course of this relationship caused her to take an overdose of Veronol that nearly killed her. True to form, upon recovering she retreated into another initially promising but ultimately unsatisfying marriage. In 1917 she married Maurice Sterne, a painter and sculptor. Shortly after they exchanged vows, however, Mabel sent Maurice packing on a honeymoon out west by himself.

Shortly after Sterne left for the Southwest, Mabel went to a medium who predicted that Indians would soon surround her. That night, Mabel had one of her legendary "psychic experiences" and saw a vision of Maurice floating above her bed, which was gradually replaced by a vision of a dark Indian face that she didn't recognize. She later said that the strange face in her vision "affected her like medicine." A few weeks later, Mabel received a prophetic letter from Maurice, urging her to come west.

Dearest Girl—

Do you want an object in life? Save the Indians, their art-culture—reveal it to the world! . . . You could, if you wanted to . . . for you have energy and are the most sensitive little girl in the world—and, above all, there is somehow a strange relationship between yourself and the Indians.

When Mabel Dodge and her son John Evans came to New Mexico in 1918, Mabel described her arrival in the Land of Enchantment as the time when she "died as an Anglo, and was reborn to a new consciousness." In her memoir, *Edge of the Taos Desert*, she described her first meeting with the Land of Enchantment this way: "My life broke in two right then, and I entered into the second half, a new world that replaced all the ways I had known with others, more strange and terrible and sweet than any I had ever been able to imagine."

Mabel's introduction into Taos society was about as rocky as the long road into the Enchanted Circle. The locals were initially suspicious of these strange New Yorkers. And because Maurice was German, he and Mabel were immediately suspected of being German spies. Mabel's love affair with the life of the pueblo, however, was instantaneous. She witnessed her first dance on the Santo Domingo pueblo on Christmas Day in 1917 and wrote:

For the first time in my life, I heard the voice of the One coming from the Many—I who until then had been taught to look for the wonders of infinite divisibility and variety, for the many in the one. . . . The singular, raging lust for individuality and separateness had been impelling me all my years as it did everyone else on earth—when all of a sudden I was brought up against the Tribe, . . . where virtue lay in wholeness instead of in dismemberment. . . . Here was a living religion that had its source in love.

In New Mexico and pueblo society's rich past, Mabel visualized America's future. Mabel's theory was that if you can construct a society in which play, religion, and work are integrated, then you have the basis for a healthier society that doesn't rape the land or exploit humanity.

Mabel began immersing herself in the culture of the Pueblo Indians. She cut off her hair and began draping herself in blankets rather than the stylish gowns of her former incarnation. She spent every spare moment among the Indians trying to get as close as possible to the tranquility of Native American village life. She also became a passionate advocate for the preservation of Pueblo culture, engaged, at the time, in an uphill battle to survive as an indigenous and unique culture.

Mabel's true rebirth to Pueblo life came when she met Antonio Luhan, a Tewa Indian, while visiting the Taos Pueblo in 1918. Tony Luhan was a towering and majestic man whose face Mabel immediately recognized as the one that had replaced Maurice's in her vision.

Mabel was immediately taken with the handsome Tewa and made arrangements for Tony to come and play the drums at her house. Tony set up a makeshift lodge on Mabel's front yard and drummed there for the better part of the spring and summer of 1918, educating Mabel in Pueblo culture and society.

Mabel was captivated with Tony, and Maurice began to get a little irritated with the growing connection between Mabel and the Tewa. Finally, fed up, Maurice stormed back to New York. Mabel and Tony began a love affair in earnest.

Inspired by her new relationship with Tony, Mabel began work on the last and the greatest of her sculpted environments, Los Gallos, or, as it came to be known later, "the Big House."

Mabel and Tony's Big House was built in Taos on the outer edge of Pueblo land. It was a sprawling hacienda reminiscent of the Medici Villa Curaria in Florence. The house had warm adobe charm, traditional arched doorways, kiva fireplaces, quiet, acacia-lined patios, and plenty of rooms to accommodate houseguests. Mabel conceived of her house as a new Eden, where she could find peace of mind and provide a safe place where others could find themselves also.

But Mabel, a restless spirit from childhood, was not built for quiet contentment. And it was very difficult for her to sit still and just enjoy Taos and Tony. Once she and Tony started living together, Mabel became convinced that Tony was holding out on her. She saw him as the man who held the key that would unlock the door to her dream of nirvana on earth. And she believed that he was refusing to give it to her.

Tony was a member of one of the most secretive and religious tribes in the region and was forbidden by tribal law to reveal any of the specifics of his religion and ritual obligations. This really irritated Mabel, who was not a woman accustomed to taking no for an answer. Her refusal to stop pressuring him resulted in violent scenes that ultimately sent Mabel packing back to New York in search of a renewed perspective.

It was at this time that Mabel went to visit Mrs. Dudley, the psychic, who reminded her of her mission and sent her back to Taos to work things out with Tony and, more importantly, with herself.

Mabel returned to Taos in 1919, married Tony, and began inviting the "great souls" that Mrs. Dudley had spoken of to spread the word about the spiritual treasures of the Southwest experience.

Celebrated artists, writers, and thinkers of the day, disenchanted with a spiritually bankrupt postwar society, flocked to Mabel and Tony Luhan's home in search of a haven that nurtured art and human nature. DH Lawrence, Andrew Dasburg, Georgia O'Keeffe, Leon Gaspard, Ansel Adams, Mary Austin, Robinson Jeffers, Laura Gilpin, Jean Toomer, Willa Cather, and many others found spiritual shelter in the Luhans' Big House.

Artists from all over the world came to the Southwest every summer to visit Mabel's desert paradise. Gradually, a form of people's art developed that was reflective of the values and visions of the region that placed people above machines and nature above profit. Mabel Luhan's tireless campaign to introduce Pueblo culture to the world encouraged understanding and appreciation for a culture that had previously been seen as a savage and backward way of life that needed to be "civilized."

Willa Cather wrote *Death Comes for the Archbishop* while in New Mexico. Ansel Adams and Laura Gilpin were inspired to spend the rest of their lives photographing the stark, southwestern landscape. Artist Georgia O'Keeffe spent the most productive years of her life in Santa Fe. John Collier, possibly the best Indian commissioner in American history, devoted the rest of his life to trying to preserve and protect Pueblo culture after Mabel showed him around her neighborhood for the first time.

Of all of the artists to whom Mabel extended an invitation to visit her Taos hacienda, D. H. Lawrence was, at least as far as Mabel was concerned, the real feather in her cap. Mabel had read

Lawrence's books and thought he was the most compelling writer in the world, and she felt that she must convince Lawrence to visit Taos at least. In order to lure him, Mabel sent Indian jewelry to Lawrence's wife, Frieda, and had Tony bless it with charms and spirits. She wrote colorful letters to Lawrence, attempting to express the spirit of the place and its people. "You must come here," she wrote. "Taos is like the dawn of the world." How could anyone, particularly Lawrence, resist a description like that?

Under the spell of Mabel Luhan's florid letters, Lawrence and Frieda arrived in Taos in 1923. They stayed briefly at Mabel's house, but ultimately Mabel made them a gift of the Kiowa Ranch, a 120-acre expanse of almost entirely vertical land balanced precariously on the northern slope of Lobo Mountain.

Lawrence loved this ranch more than any other place that he had lived, and his failing health improved considerably as he worked with the Indians, mended roofs, and built his outdoor oven. Like most of her close associations, Mabel's relationship with the Lawrences was intense. Mabel was a woman who could demonstrate great generosity and devotion and could just as easily whip up an emotional hurricane when she was of a mind to.

Despite her magnetism Mabel was a difficult woman who simultaneously attracted and repelled the people she invited into her home. She could just as easily drive someone away as bring him or her close, and she was very manipulative. There was often a lot of tension and anger in her household. At these moments the Big House was definitely not a paradise on earth.

But this was perhaps part of the reason why so much classic work was generated in Mabel's garden. If the Big House truly had been some kind of paradise where people just laid around in the sun, it probably would never have generated the kind of creativity that it ultimately produced. Creativity arises as much out of

Tony Luhan

tension and conflict as out of ease and serenity. The fusion physics of contact between two strong and opposing points of view is an important element in any lasting artistic or philosophical movement.

Mabel spent the rest of her life in Taos. While her later years were more sedate, and though the world grew less passionate about her message of a return to the virtues of tribal simplicity, Mabel continued to live and love the Taos area in many significant and lasting ways. Mabel built the town's first hospital, donated thousands of dollars worth of books to the local library, and was a steadfast and compassionate champion for the rights of the Indian tribes of the Southwest.

Mabel and Tony spent their last years surrounded by their close friends—Robinson Jeffers, Dorothy Brett, Frieda Lawrence, and John Evans's daughter Bonnie, who visited the Big House every summer.

Mabel died in her beloved Taos on August 13, 1962. After Mabel's funeral, Dorothy Brett wrote to Bonnie, describing the service this way:

> I wonder if anyone has described to you the extraordinary fitness and beauty of Mabel's funeral . . . for some obscure reason, Mabel's was not grim. Even the service in the church . . . was so simple and clear-cut, that there was no female hysteria, nor to me sadness. The amazing beauty lay in the Cemetery, the Kit Carson Cemetery, under the large Cottonwood trees. The heavy greens, flashing sunlight, was so peaceful and happy. The grave was in a corner, along the fences stood large sheaves of gladiolas, scarlet, orange, yellow, white, perfectly lovely. Four sisters in pure white stood watching. On the polished mahogany coffin lay a sheaf of shining

gladiolas. . . . It was so perfect, so Mabelish . . . I felt she was where she would want to be, in a shady garden.

Tony died a year later, and the house, as if it had by osmosis absorbed some of Mabel's magnetic spirit, continued to be a gathering place for revolutionary thinkers and artists.

Actor Dennis Hopper bought Los Gallos in the 1960s, and it is now a bed and breakfast where travelers are introduced to the magical and transforming influences of Mabel's garden.

Bonnie Evans later described Mabel as "truly rich, as a landscape or a tapestry can be . . . she was able to create a physical and emotional arena in which people found the energy to act." Mabel had the courage and the creativity to see her world in an original way. She dispensed with the blurred outlines and faded colors of conventional wisdom and dared to be reborn to beauty and, as a consequence, enriched the world. In this sense Mabel Dodge Luhan truly was an artist of life.

FRIEDA LAWRENCE
1879–1956

A Genius for Living

*B*aroness Frieda von Richtofen Weekley stood in front of her home's French windows on a bright, sunny Easter morning in 1912. A soft breeze fluttered the curtains as her three children laughed and hunted for Easter eggs in the back garden. By all accounts she could be counted a lucky woman. She was married to a university professor and had a fine home in a fine town and three beautiful children. She had everything that an upper-middle-class suburban woman in 1912 could hope for.

And yet Frieda was growing increasingly restless and dissatisfied. Her husband, an earnest professor of languages, was far more conventional and proper than she. He couldn't hope to match the force of Frieda's spirit or her appetite for life. Lately, Frieda had been searching for something to fill the void she felt with her carefully measured life. And then, D. H. Lawrence walked into her parlor, and she knew that she had met her soul mate: "I see him before me as he entered the house. A long, thin figure, quick, straight legs, light, sure movements. He seemed so obviously simple. Yet he arrested my attention. There was something more than met the eye. What kind of a bird was this?"

Frieda and D. H. Lawrence, a young English novelist then a student of her husband's, felt an immediate kinship such as Frieda had never experienced with her reserved and proper husband.

And so it is no surprise that after only a few meetings, Frieda and D. H. Lawrence fell in love. Shortly thereafter, on May 3, 1912, Frieda left her husband and her children behind and ran away with Lawrence. It was the most fulfilling and also the most heartbreaking decision she made in her life, but she had heard the voice of her own destiny, and she followed it. She said later:

> I was frightened. I knew how terrible such a thing would be for my husband. He had always trusted me. But a force stronger than myself made me deal him the blow. I left the next day. I left my son with his father, my two little girls I took to their grandparents in London. I said goodbye to them on the Hampstead Heath, blind and blank with pain, dimly feeling I should never again live with them as I had done. Lawrence met me at Charing Cross Station, to go away with him, never to leave him again. He seemed to have lifted me body and soul out of all my past life. This young man of twenty-six had taken all my fate, all my destiny, into his hands. And we had known each other barely for six weeks. There had been nothing else for me to do but submit.

Thus began a legendary eighteen-year love affair between two philosophical adventurers, who together explored the uncharted regions of love and intimacy, attempting to reintroduce sensuality, humanity, and organic sympathy into an increasingly alienated and industrialized world.

Frieda and D. H. Lawrence with unidentified person

Frieda Lawrence is an ambiguous figure in women's history because she didn't create art herself but let her vision and talent speak through a man. This was not unusual for women of her era. In 1912 many intelligent and ambitious women still remained in the background, influencing the world indirectly through the vehicle of a powerful man. And even Frieda's most stunning creation—her love for Lawrence—was shrouded in scandal from the very beginning. Frieda, after all, was married when she met D. H. Lawrence, and German divorce law required her to leave her children with her husband when she eloped with Lawrence.

But when we see Frieda Lawrence in the context of her own life, we begin to understand what a courageous and inspiring woman she really was and how her life is a lesson for all of us in how to find the strength and grace to be who we are. For better or worse, Frieda was a woman who wasn't afraid to speak up and act out; as such, she helped pave the way for all women to defy social conventions and, as Frieda put it, "live in greater depth."

Frieda Lawrence was the second of three daughters born to Baron Friedrich von Richthofen and Anna Marquier von Richthofen. Frieda, as the family tomboy, was very close to her father, who had a commanding presence. He had been an officer in the Franco-Prussian War. A war injury left him unfit for military service, and by the time Frieda came along, he had become a disappointed civil servant with a penchant for risky business deals. He squandered away most of his family fortune.

As a consequence there was no dowry for his three daughters, and Frieda was encouraged to look early and look hard for a husband to care for her. So when Frieda met Ernest Weekley in July of 1898 while on a vacation in the Black Forest with her family, she set her cap for him on the spot.

Ernest Weekley was a conservative and studious language professor at University College in Nottingham. Weekley was fifteen years older than Frieda and far more conventional and staid, but he was taken with Frieda's robust beauty and fertile mind. He fell in love with her at first sight. And for Frieida's part, she sensed a solid moral core in Weekley, and his dependability appealed to a woman who had been raised with such uncertainty surrounding her. Frieda and Weekley were married on August 29, 1899.

It became immediately apparent to Frieda that she and Ernest were not going to be very compatible mates. Ernest was much less intense than Frieda, and, in fact, seemed to be a little frightened by her. It is said that on their wedding night, as Frieda sensually descended the stairs toward him, he shrank from her and rushed out of his study, declaring, "My God, I have married an earthquake." Little did he know how prophetic his words would turn out to be.

The couple settled into a sedate and comfortable life in Mapperley, just outside Nottingham. Frieda struggled to fill the role of a middle-class suburban housewife at the turn of the century. She supervised the household, shopped, and paid visits to friends. To keep her mind active, she read voraciously and edited German textbooks. Frieda and Ernest's first child, Charles Montague, was born in June of 1900, followed by Elsa Agnes Frieda in September 1902 and Barbara Joy in October 1904.

Despite the joy she found in her children, Frieda became increasingly restless with her life. She was starving for passion and experience and desperate to expand her horizons. To relieve her restlessness, Frieda had a series of affairs, first with Will Downson, a lace manufacturer, and later with Otto Gross, a prominent German physician who had studied under Freud. But then, in the spring of 1912, a former student of her husband's, D. H. Lawrence, walked into her parlor, and Frieda's life changed forever.

When Lawrence entered her life, Frieda was thirty-one and

Lawrence twenty-six. They felt an immediate kinship. After their first meeting it is said that Lawrence sent Frieda a note calling her the most "wonderful woman in the world." These must have been welcome words indeed for a woman whose husband had compared her to a natural disaster on their wedding night. Just a few short months after their first meeting, Frieda left her husband, her home, and her children to wander the world with Lawrence. They would be virtually inseparable for the next eighteen years.

Despite her love for Lawrence, however, Frieda was tormented by the separation from her young children. Throughout 1913 and 1914 she begged Weekley for a chance to see them, but Ernest, who never forgave Frieda for her betrayal, refused to allow her any contact. Her grief was compounded by the fact that Lawrence, perhaps out of a sense of guilt for causing the separation or perhaps because of jealousy, had no tolerance for Frieda's pain and offered little support or assistance.

In May of 1914 Frieda's divorce from Weekley became final, and as the German courts of that day gave full custody to the father when a wife broke her marriage vows, her separation from her children became formalized by law. Her contact with her children was left entirely up to Ernest's discretion until they came of age. Ernest kept the children far away from Frieda and told the children that their mother had left them and disgraced the family. He spent the rest of his life nursing a broken heart. Frieda's daughter Barbara said later: "When I told Frieda how my father would refer to 'his tragedy' Frieda said, 'What's he going to do with his tragedy when he dies, leave it to Uncle George in his will?'"

Although Frieda was sensitive to Ernest's pain, she also resented the way he embraced his suffering like a best friend and used his martyrdom as a weapon against her. Frieda was a resilient woman who rebounded from adversity, and despite her sometimes great suffering, she always found a way to say yes to life. Ernest's commitment to his pain must have seemed to her like yet another example of Weekley's inability to match the strength and exuberance of her spirit.

When it became apparent to Frieda that she was not going to be allowed in her children's lives, she left with Lawrence to wander Europe in search of a freer and deeper lifestyle based on truth, beauty, and love. When the war came, because Frieda was German, Frieda and Lawrence were suspected of being German spies, and they were expelled from Cornwall, England. Eventually, they moved south, spending the years from 1917 to 1921 living throughout Italy. Then, on August 10, 1922, Frieda and Lawrence sailed for America at the invitation of Mabel Dodge Luhan, to live in Taos, New Mexico.

Mabel Dodge Luhan, a famous American hostess, had dedicated herself to starting a new school of enlightenment in Taos, New Mexico. She attracted some of the greatest minds of her day to the region, and D. H. Lawrence, literature's "priest of love," was the one person she most wanted to join her in Taos. So Mabel Dodge Luhan set about trying to convince the Lawrences to resettle in her house in Taos, New Mexico. She sent Lawrence compelling descriptions about the organic, earth-centered beauty of pueblo life and gave Frieda lavish Indian jewelry.

By 1925 Lawrence, who was chronically ill, had been diagnosed with tuberculosis, and Frieda and Lawrence settled full-time at Mabel's Kiowa Ranch above Taos, New Mexico. The Lawrences had finally found a home in this spiritual mecca, and although they lived there together for only a few years, their presence has greatly influenced and increased the spiritual mystique and popularity of the area.

Lawrence died in France on March 2, 1930. He was buried in Venice, but his ashes were later moved to a chapel in Taos built by Frieda's lover, Antonio Ravagli, where they rest to this day. *Not*

Mabel Dodge Luhan, Frieda Lawrence, and artist Dorothy Brett
(left to right)

I, but the Wind, Frieda's memoir of life with D. H. Lawrence, was published in 1934.

Frieda married Ravagli in 1950, but their relation bore none of the earmarks of the great love affair Frieda had enjoyed with Lawrence. Their marriage seemed rather to be a business arrangement between two consulting and amicable comrades. Frieda made a final visit to England in 1952 to visit her children and meet her grandchildren.

Frieda died on August 11, 1956, on her seventy-seventh birthday, and was buried beside Lawrence in their memorial shrine. Frieda's autobiography, *And the Fullness Thereof*, which she had been slowly pulling together over several years, was published posthumously in 1964 as *Frieda Lawrence, the Memoirs and Correspondence*.

The quality of the love between Frieda and D. H. Lawrence and the courage of their life together was to be Frieda Lawrence's primary accomplishment. She had what Lawrence referred to as a "genius for living" as well as a great capacity for love and an unquenchable appetite for life, which was at the heart of the spiritual and philosophical messages in Lawrence's fiction. Frieda is at the center of *Lady Chatterley's Lover, The Rainbow, Aaron's Rod,* and many of Lawrence's timeless masterpieces that espouse a life of body and spirit and a connection with nature. Frieda's "genius for living" and her enormous capacity for love can perhaps inspire us to change the way we love one another and ourselves.

MARIA MARTINEZ
1887–1980

Master Potter of San Ildefonso

*M*aria Martinez told her husband, Julian, to add another log to the hardwood blaze in which their pots were firing. Julian added the log, and the fire leapt and snapped in the crisp desert air. Maria could sense that the flame had grown too intense and that the pots that they had so carefully molded, designed, and polished were in danger of cracking. Maria motioned to Julian, and he threw a large amount of manure over the roaring flame, snuffing it out instantly.

Little did Maria or Julian know that by dousing an out-of-control flame, they had just invented a whole new form of pottery. When Maria and Julian recovered their pots, they were not cracked as they had feared they would be. But the red clay had turned completely black.

Maria, who was nothing if not resourceful, decorated the pots with black paint and showed the black-on-black pots to a trader who arrived a few days later. The Anglo world had suddenly taken an interest in Native American pottery, and the traders came more and more frequently to buy from the Pueblo artists. Maria

Maria Martinez displaying some of her pottery

led the trader to the storeroom and showed him the blackened pots. She explained that these were "special" pots that they did not usually sell, so she would have to charge more.

The trader agreed to buy every single pot for top dollar, and a short time later he returned and asked Maria and Julian for more of the black-on-black pots. Soon, Maria and Julian taught the other San Ildefonso potters this new method of pottery making, and the villagers began selling as many pots as they could produce.

Through a happy disaster, Maria Martinez had found a new form of pottery that would become accepted and popularized as the "authentic" traditional pottery of San Ildefonso, which, of course, it wasn't. But Maria had done even more than this. She had found a way for this part of her culture as well as her community to survive in a modern world.

At the turn of the century, a band of preservationists, predominantly Anglo women who regarded Pueblo culture as a model society, dedicated themselves to the preservation of the Pueblo culture's arts and ideals. Although their intentions were probably good, their insistence upon a very personal and some-what romantic vision of what constituted authentic Native American culture oftentimes compromised the Pueblo culture's ability to grow and adapt to contemporary society.

With her pottery Maria found a way to satisfy the preservationist's appetite for authenticity while at the same time allowing San Ildefonso to continue its pursuit of cultural arts and to make money. And, as was Pueblo tradition, Maria shared her success with her village however she could.

When Maria and Julian bought their first car—a Dodge sedan—Julian made it into a piece of sacred art, adorning it with Indian designs. They allowed people from the pueblo to use the car, and it became the "San Ildefonso Dodge." Maria once told one of her interviewers: "That was the first car in the pueblo . . .

It was a black car, all black. I can see the designs Julian put on that car. He painted it all around just like pots. You would be surprised what I would do with that car. We took everybody who was sick. And we'd get food. We helped everybody with that car."

It is estimated that Maria Antonia Montoya was born on the San Ildefonso pueblo in 1887. And for all of her nearly one hundred years, she lived at San Ildefonso, sharing her craft with others and doing what she could for her community. San Ildefonso is a peaceful, rural community located some 20 miles northwest of Santa Fe, New Mexico. A Tewa-speaking tribe first inhabited the area around A.D. 1300, and since then the pueblo has undergone many transformations as a consequence of first Spanish and later Anglo intervention.

Maria became a potter when she was just a little girl. She learned from her aunt, who was a well-respected potter. The aunt would work after dinner each night, teaching little Maria how to pinch the pots and prepare them for firing.

Maria Montoya married Julian Martinez around 1908. By this time she was already a noteworthy potter, and shortly after her marriage, she was asked by Dr. Edgar Lee Hewett, then the director of the Museum of New Mexico, to produce some polychrome pots that were made using ancient San Ildefonso techniques for the museum. Examples of these techniques had been discovered in an excavation of an ancient pueblo close to San Ildefonso. Maria shaped the pots the way her aunt had taught her, and Julian painted them. Thus began the lifelong creative collaboration that produced some of the world's finest pots.

To make a pot, Maria would make a pancake of clay to form the base, then carefully coil the clay around the base to form the walls of the pot. When Maria got the shape she wanted, she smoothed the clay with pieces of gourd and then polished the clay with a stone before the red slip was completely dry. Next, Julian would paint decorations on the polished surface, and, like Maria, he combined the ancient with the contemporary, using prehistoric designs in new combinations. Finally, the pots would be fired.

Maria and Julian refined their pottery techniques, and when their black-on-black ware became more well known, they were invited to demonstrate their craft at the 1904 St. Louis World's Fair, the 1914 Panama-California Exposition in San Diego, and the 1934 Chicago World's Fair.

Maria and Julian's creative use of matte and gloss finishes to create the unique, multilayered, black-on-black effect made their pottery world famous. But part of what is so special about San Ildefonso pottery is the San Ildefonso clay itself. Every pueblo mines clay from its own tribal land. And every pueblo's clay is different. San Ildefonso clay is mixed with volcanic ash and is harvested from a variety of areas in small batches, giving the clay a mineral diversity that adds texture and color to the earthenware. It also has a high iron content, which turns the pots black as they're firing.

Maria and Julian produced pottery together for forty years, while participating in their village and raising a family in the San Ildefonso tradition. Their sons and daughters watched their parents work together to make their signature earthenware and carried on the tradition after their parents were gone.

After Julian's death in 1943, Maria began working with her daughter-in-law, Santana. Santana provided the painted decorations that had been her father-in-law's legacy. After 1956 Maria also worked with her son, Popovi Da, who was instrumental in marketing Maria's work and who even built a shop at the pueblo. Popovi Da gave lectures across the country, spreading the word about the San Ildefonso style. One of the family's most talented and noteworthy potters is Maria's grandson Tony Da. Following in his mother's tradition, Tony combined the techniques he learned from his grandparents and parents and mixed them with new sculptural techniques to create a whole new form of contemporary San Ildefonso pottery.

At present many other family members and people from San Ildefonso have carried on Maria's style of black-on-black pottery. Maria died in 1980, leaving a legacy of new/old pottery that has carried her culture and her craft into the modern world.

GEORGIA O'KEEFFE

1887–1986

A Woman on Paper

Georgia O'Keeffe was sitting quietly at a table in the cafeteria of the Columbia University Teachers College when an excited woman rushed up to her and asked her if her name was Virginia O'Keeffe. Georgia shook her head that it was not, and the woman told her it was a pity, because there was the most extraordinary show of paintings at Stieglitz's Gallery 291, all done by a woman named Virginia O'Keeffe. Georgia resolved to pay a visit to Alfred Stieglitz's renowned gallery that very day, and see this Virginia O'Keeffe's remarkable drawings.

As Georgia walked up the stairs and into the main room of the stately Gallery 291, she could hardy believe her eyes. There, arranged with care and precision and magnificently complimented by the period architecture of the brownstone walls, were her deeply personal drawings. Alfred Stieglitz, the gallery owner, had put her drawings on display without her permission and without even using her correct name!

Georgia O'Keeffe

"For me," Georgia O'Keeffe later wrote in her autobiography, "the drawings were private and the idea of their being on the wall for the public to look at was just too much."

Georgia demanded to see Stieglitz immediately, but the gallery owner was away on jury duty. Unable to give Stieglitz a piece of her mind right there and then, Georgia decided to take a look around, and despite herself, she realized that her drawings had been hung with a great deal of sensitivity and understanding. But this shouldn't have come as any surprise to Georgia. Georgia had first encountered Stieglitz in 1907, while she was a student at the Art Students League in New York. At that time Stieglitz, who was himself a photographer of some note, was one of the first gallery owners to assert that photography was a serious art form. Throughout the next eleven years, Stieglitz continued his tradition of introducing the public to innovative and important art. In fact, it was in Gallery 291 that Americans first saw the paintings of such modern European masters as Pablo Picasso and Paul Cézanne.

So despite her irritation, Georgia's drawings were in good company, and Georgia knew it. Some years earlier, Georgia had confided to her friend and fellow-artist Anita Pollitzer, "I believe I would rather have Stieglitz like something—anything I have done—than anyone else I know of."

As a consequence of those words, spoken so many years before to her friend, Georgia's drawings came to be hung in Gallery 291. Georgia had sent her charcoal drawings to Pollitzer while she was teaching in South Carolina. They represented a departure from her usual style and she wanted Anita's opinion. Anita admired the drawings, and knowing how timid Georgia could be, took the drawings to Stieglitz. It is said that Stieglitz examined them closely and then declared, "At last, a woman on paper!"

A week after Georgia first discovered her work hanging in Gallery 291, she returned to confront Stieglitz. She found him in the rear of the gallery. Stieglitz was an intense man with a great shock of white hair and a large mustache. Georgia thought he seemed to look right through her.

Georgia, who cut a stark and intense figure herself in her severe black dress and Spartan white collar, marched up to Stieglitz and demanded that he take down her drawings immediately. Stieglitz refused, saying that he wanted them on the wall so that he could look at them often. Georgia, who had come to give him what-for, wound up telling Stieglitz she'd be pleased to have Gallery 291 display her drawings. Thus began the antagonistic solidarity that typified their long and intense relationship. Alfred Stieglitz and Georgia O'Keeffe would be married just a few years later.

Before he became her husband, however, Stieglitz became Georgia's creative champion. The art community in the early 1900s did not take women artists very seriously. True to his trailblazing nature, however, Stieglitz felt that women had something important, something fiercely personal and fundamentally different to offer American culture. So his choice to display Georgia's powerful drawings was no accident. He knew that it would shake up the art world, and he was right.

Georgia's drawings caused a sensation, and critics and prominent artists filled the gallery during the coming months to see these powerful and sensual drawings done by an unknown female art teacher.

Disturbed by their sensuality and honesty, art critic Willard H. Wright is said to have complained to Stieglitz, "All these pictures say is 'I want to have a baby.'"

"That's fine," Stieglitz replied. "A woman has painted a picture telling you that she wants to have a baby." Long a defender of creative freedom, Stieglitz thought that the sexual expressiveness of Georgia's work was just what a sexually repressed America needed.

Georgia's groundbreaking show at Gallery 291 ran from April until July 1917. Georgia had returned to the University of Virginia to teach summer school by then, but she had left New York with a new sense of momentum and optimism. Thanks to Stieglitz and the quality of her stunning charcoals, the years of work, study, and stubborn commitment had finally begun to pay off. Georgia's drawings had at last been displayed in public, and they had created a sensation.

Georgia O'Keeffe was born on November 18, 1887, outside Sun Prairie, Wisconsin. When Georgia was eleven, her mother enrolled her in art classes, and by the time Georgia was in the eighth grade, she had already decided that when she grew up, she would become an artist. This was a very unorthodox idea for a little girl growing up at the turn of the century. At this time women were discouraged from pursuing careers of any kind, let alone a career in the arts.

But this wasn't the first time Georgia had rocked the boat, and her family had grown used to Georgia's unorthodox ideas. Georgia, an iconoclast from an early age, spent a lot of her time defying convention. If her sisters braided their hair, she wore hers down. If they wore bonnets and bows, she chose to be plain. And most shockingly of all, Georgia could run faster and jump higher than most of the boys!

Georgia's family believed in education for boys and girls, and they encouraged Georgia to keep up with her art classes. Georgia's mother tried to temper her daughter's eventual disappointment, however, by explaining that the best Georgia could realistically hope for was to become an art teacher. But deep down inside, Georgia knew that she was headed for a much larger arena than the classroom. And she intended to prove it.

In 1903 the O'Keeffe family relocated to Virginia. Georgia continued to take private art lessons, and after graduating from high school, she attended the Art Institute of Chicago. The following year Georgia came down with typhoid fever. After she recovered, Georgia enrolled at the Art Students League in New York City in 1907. By 1908, however, perhaps fearing that her family's prediction about her becoming an art teacher rather than an artist would come true, she chose not to return to school, instead accepting a position as a commercial artist in Chicago.

Although she had managed to elude the fate that society had predicted for her, Georgia was dissatisfied with life in the advertising industry, which left her little time for her personal painting. Georgia left advertising that year and accepted a position as a drawing instructor in Amarillo, Texas. During the summers she traveled back to her home to take classes and later work at the University of Virginia. This would begin a lifelong theme for Georgia, who spent most of her life with her time and heart divided between two locations.

In 1914 Georgia was back in New York, taking classes at Teachers College. In the fall of 1915, she began teaching art at Columbia College in South Carolina. Around this time she mailed a series of charcoal drawings to Anita Pollitzer, which led to Georgia's encounter with Stieglitz at Gallery 291.

In 1917 Georgia became ill, and Stieglitz urged her to take a leave of absence from her teaching and come back to New York. Georgia moved into a large, sunny room in a brownstone belonging to Alfred Stieglitz's brother Leopold. Gallery 291 had closed due to financial pressure, so Alfred had established a studio and gallery on the fourth floor of his brother's home. He installed Georgia on the third floor. And there at last, in her urban sanctuary under Stieglitz's protection, Georgia began to paint full-time, finally becoming the artist that she had always dreamed of being.

While Georgia painted, Stieglitz arranged showings of her paintings in the most influential galleries, exercising meticulous care when selecting the lucky few who could become collectors of Georgia's work. Rather than grooming her to be a schoolteacher, Stieglitz was positioning Georgia to become one of the most prominent and well-respected living American artists. And for a woman painter in the 1920s, that was nothing short of a miracle.

During this exciting period Georgia began what was to be one of her most prolific and successful themes. In the midst of New York City, far removed from the epic and organic sweep of her native landscape, Georgia began to paint flowers.

Why would an artist paint flowers in the middle of New York City? This is how Georgia herself explained it: "Most people in the city rush around so, they have no time to look at a flower. I want them to see it whether they want to or not."

In 1924 Stieglitz arranged the first showing of Georgia's paintings at the prestigious Anderson Galleries. More than 500 people per day visited the gallery, and the word on the street was that O'Keeffe was a triumph. Unfortunately, the critics weren't as kind, but by Georgia's second showing in the spring of 1924, which presented fifty-one paintings including, for the first time, those magnificent flowers, the press was trumpeting her praises. Georgia and Stieglitz had taken the art world by storm. They were now an indivisible team, and in December, Georgia O'Keeffe and Alfred Stieglitz were married.

The demand for Georgia's work, and thus the pressure to produce, increased dramatically. Georgia, growing tired of the urban landscape that surrounded her, sought out new territory. On the advice of friends, Georgia traveled to Taos, New Mexico, and stayed in the home of the legendary Mabel Dodge Luhan. Mabel's Big House had become a spiritual and creative mecca for artists, thinkers, and others in search of a new awakening.

Georgia fell instantly in love with this enchanted land of vast expanses, lyrical peaks, and ancient cultures. She began spending more and more of her time away from Stieglitz, exploring the southwestern desert.

Georgia navigated the back roads of New Mexico in a Model A Ford, and it is said that she was undaunted by her frightened driving teachers, who told her she was the worst driver they had ever seen. Unconcerned, Georgia drove through the desert she was growing to love, stopping frequently to paint what she saw, using the unbolted front seat of her Model A as an easel.

From 1929 onward Georgia was spending half of her time in New Mexico. She painted the swelling arroyos and red peaks and sun-bleached bones of the desert. When she returned to spend time with Stieglitz, she would ship back crates of desert artifacts so that she could continue to paint New Mexico from Stieglitz's summer home in Lake George, New York.

In 1945 Georgia bought an abandoned hacienda called the Ghost Ranch in Abiquiu, New Mexico, just outside Santa Fe. Georgia purchased the house because she fell in love with the simple adobe architecture and the view of the mesa along the Jemez Range, which would figure prominently in her future work. "It's my private mountain," Georgia is claimed to have said. "It belongs to me. God told me if I painted it enough, I could have it."

In 1946 Stieglitz suffered a cerebral thrombosis, and Georgia flew to New York to be by his side. Alfred Stieglitz, who had been a good deal older than Georgia, died on July 13, 1946.

Georgia spent the next three winters in New York settling Stieglitz's estate and learning how to handle the business responsibilities of her own career, which Stieglitz had always attended to for her.

"For me he was much more wonderful in his work than as a human being," Georgia said after his death. "I believe it was the work that kept me with him. . . . though I loved him . . . as a human being . . . I put up with what seemed to me a good deal of contradictory nonsense because of what seemed clear and bright and wonderful."

Although the loss of Stieglitz was difficult for Georgia, she was comforted by the fact that she no longer had to live a life divided by her allegiance to Stieglitz and her love of the Southwest. She moved into the Ghost Ranch full-time and spent most of her time painting the adobe architecture and turquoise doors of her home.

Georgia had a major retrospective at the Art Institute of Chicago in 1943 and later an exhibit at the Museum of Modern Art. In the 1950s Georgia fell out of fashion and had only three solo showings in the decade.

Georgia settled into a life outside the spotlight, enjoying her home and her garden in Abiquiu and traveling extensively. But Georgia, much like the perennial flowers that had made her famous, blossomed once more, and by the 1970s public attention turned once again toward Georgia's paintings. She was invited to show at the Whitney in New York, and the grand O'Keeffe retrospective, which traveled to the Art Institute of Chicago and the San Francisco Museum of Art, set new attendance records.

In 1971, when she was eighty-four years old, Georgia's eyesight began to fail, and in 1972 she stopped painting altogether. Juan Hamilton, a young potter, knocked on Georgia's door one day looking for work, and the two became partners. Georgia learned pottery from Juan, letting her fingers see what her eyes could not. Juan became Georgia's companion and business manager until her death.

Georgia died on March 6, 1986, at the age of ninety-eight. Per her instructions she was cremated, and Juan scattered her ashes from the summit of her beloved Pedernal Mountain in New Mexico.

For Georgia a lily was not just a lily but also a reminder of the procreative and creative yearnings of nature. To her, bleached desert bones "seem to cut sharply to the center of something that is keenly alive on the desert even tho' it is vast and empty and untouchable . . . and knows no kindness with all its beauty."

Georgia O'Keeffe's paintings help us all to appreciate the beauty of the world around us and to glimpse the creative power of the universe in the stamen of a single springtime flower.

LAURA GILPIN

1891–1979

Cowgirl at Heart

*E*ighty-eight-year-old Laura Gilpin gripped her camera with aging but still steady hands, leaning as far as she could out of the small plane that carried her over the 250,000 acres of Navajo land that had become her adopted homeland. The tiny craft's wings dipped in the desert wind, seeming to almost lightly kiss the top branches of the piñon and cedar trees that dotted the landscape she had loved and photographed for nearly sixty years.

Laura had spent her life trying to capture and communicate the emotion of the deeply carved chasms of the Canyon De Chelly, the awesome limitlessness of the northern New Mexico desert, and the conquered but enduring nobility of the vanishing Rio Grande snaking its way tentatively southward, to "surrender its surplus to the sea." Laura Gilpin's photographs of the great Southwest helped others see through her eyes and understand what she considered the beating heart of the natural world, the timelessness of the terrain, and humanity's fleeting but inextricable connection to nature.

"In this great southwest," as Laura herself explains in her book, *The Pueblos: A Camera Chronicle*, "the vast landscape plays an all-important part in the lives of its people. Their architecture resembles the giant erosions of nature's carving. It is a land of contrasts, of gentleness and warmth, and fierce and raging storms; of timbered mountains and verdant valleys, and wide, arid desert; of gayety and song, and cruel strife."

Laura Gilpin got her first camera, a Kodak Brownie, as a present for her twelfth birthday. By age seventeen she was experimenting with autochrome and beginning to establish the very first cornerstones of her unique niche in the history of photography and of New Mexico. Laura was interested in the region as a maternal force that guided and defined the lives of the people who lived there. To her a photograph should not only document the land but also reflect its inner beauty. This idea was already a departure from the reality-based, male-dominated tradition of photography at that time.

Laura's male counterparts, such as Ansel Adams or such nineteenth-century photographer explorers as William Henry Jackson (to whom Laura was distantly related), photographed the West as a place of inviolate, pristine beauty, untouched by human habitation. For Laura the southwestern desert was not an unpolished jewel either awaiting or resisting the intrusion of human development, but a populated land rich with history and tradition inextricably bound up with the people who lived there. As Ansel Adams said after her death, she had "a highly individualistic eye. I don't have the sense that she was influenced except by the land itself."

Laura Gilpin's view of the landscapes she photographed take into account the human and emotional elements invoked by nature and, in so doing, have created a uniquely feminine vision of the terrain. Although she worked in a field traditionally dominated by men and in her own life insisted that her work was genderless, Gilpin's interpretations of the natural world, like some women

"Indian family, Acoma pueblo," photo by Laura Gilpin

writers of her day such as Willa Cather, give a highly personal and human account of the landscape.

Despite her reputation as a "feminine" photographer, Laura Gilpin was intimately connected to the male tradition of western landscape photography. American landscape photography grew as a natural extension of the government survey teams that went west in the 1860s and 1870s to capture accurate images of the undeveloped American frontier. Photography was a physically challenging business in those days, not only because of the remoteness of the areas but because of the equipment the art required.

A person needed hundreds of pounds of equipment, gallons of chemicals and fresh water for development, and fragile glass-plate negatives to create a photograph. All of this had to be hauled up mountains and across vast, arid desert expanses in order to capture an image. It was a difficult and a lonely profession, requiring a good deal of grit and a thirst for adventure that was stronger than the need for human companionship. Most early explorer/photographers were spirited and independent men who were willing to spend many months away from their families and the comforts of home. A veteran of two decades of exploration photography, Carleton Watkins, complained to his wife in 1882, "I have never had the time seem so long to me on any trip I ever made from home, and I am not half done with my work. . . . It drags along awful slow, between the smoke and the rain and the wind, and as if the elements were not enough to worry me, a spark from an engine set fire to my . . . tent last week and burned it half up."

Survey photographers like Jackson or Watkins who photographed the West did not think of themselves as artists. They were surveyors, recording accurate photographic data that reflected what their government and railroad employers wanted to see: an expansive and inviting new land, unpopulated, and welcoming commercial development. Although these photographers made pictures of great beauty, their chief purpose was to document the land in the interests of American settlement.

All of this isolation and backbreaking enterprise would have seemed a strange path indeed for a young woman of Laura's generation to choose. But Laura was not an average young woman. Laura Gilpin grew up appreciating the rough and ready splendor of the West, and throughout her life remained a cowgirl at heart. She could camp out in the woods for days on end or lean out of an airplane at eighty-eight years of age if it meant getting the picture that she wanted. And she was a woman who could tolerate solitude. Laura worked for most of her life in virtual isolation, waiting in the silent, remote regions of the Southwest to hear the desert whisper its secrets to her.

Laura Gilpin was born in 1891 just outside Colorado Springs. She was distantly related to William Gilpin, the visionary expansionist and explorer who became Colorado's first territorial governor, and to the photographer William Henry Jackson. So she had, embedded in her genealogical history, the combination of pioneer and photographer that would steer her course.

As a girl, she knew Dr. William A. Bell, who had photographed along the thirty-second parallel for the Kansas Pacific Railroad in 1867. She was also a friend of General William Jackson Palmer, founder of the Denver and Rio Grande Railroad and to whom she herself accredited her lifelong love affair with the geography of the West.

Laura Gilpin's father, Frank, was a scion of Baltimore society with a misplaced love of the open range. He, like a lot of young men of his generation, went west, moving to Colorado in 1880 to seek his fortune. He tried his hand at ranching, mining, and investing before settling down to a career as a fine furniture maker in the late 1920s.

Laura's mother, Emma Miller Gilpin, did not share her husband's enthusiasm for the unwashed and, as far as she was concerned, uncivilized Southwest. Emma was from a prominent St. Louis family, and although she followed her husband west, she always tried to bring her love of Eastern refinement and culture into the family's rustic homelife. She encouraged Laura to study music and art and insisted that her daughter be educated at the finest East Coast boarding schools. But Laura, who was much more in tune with her father's wide-ranging sensibilities, felt out of place in the traditional Eastern boarding-school setting that backdropped her life from 1905 until 1909, and she was rumored to have asserted her unique spirit by showing up at cotillions in cowboy outfits. Eventually she was allowed to come back to the West that she loved.

In 1916, after experimenting with photography for more than a decade, Laura Gilpin left the West once more and moved to New York to study photographic pictorialism at the Clarence H. White School. Rather like the impressionists' influence upon painting as a medium, pictorialists emphasized feeling and emotion rather than accurate physical description. Pictorialism was characterized by soft-focus-lens views of a hazy, romanticized world that appealed to Laura, and negatives and prints were manipulated to produce a more atmospheric and evocative image. They were an important step away from the work of survey photographers and toward a more artistic vision of photography.

Laura returned to the Southwest a year later, profoundly influenced by White's pictorial style. Her own creative inclinations had been radicalized by White's idea of photography as an art form. Years after, Laura recalled White's influence on her: "Many enter the field of photography with the impulse to record a scene. They often fail to realize that what they wish to do is to record the emotion felt upon viewing that scene. . . . a mere record photograph in no way reflects that emotion."

Shortly after her return to Colorado, Laura opened a commercial studio specializing in portraiture and began taking pictures of the nearby mountains and prairies of eastern Colorado. Her work won some early accolades in the press, most notably her picture of the Colorado prairie, which New York critics praised as giving "most successfully the sense of the vastness of the plains." Whereas a single tree or outcropping might represent an entire mountain range for documentary photographers, Laura focused on the big picture. Laura wanted to suggest the vast and mythic expanse of the place—the majestic scale of nature—so that she could better suggest the sweep of human history and the impact of the environment on patterns of human settlement.

Guided by this vision, in the 1920s Laura became increasingly interested in the rich historical legacy of the Southwest. She made her first trip to Mesa Verde in 1924 and tried to express through her photographs the tentative but enduring culture of the ancient cliff dwellers. The spare simplicity of their lives intrigued Laura, and the pictures she took at this time were soft-focus, evocative images that suggested the romantic spirit of the place.

As Martha Sandweiss, in her essay "Laura Gilpin and the Tradition of American Landscape Photography," explains it:

Gilpin's broad, emotional response to Mesa Verde [she returned in 1925] was much like that of Willa Cather, whose story about the discovery of the ruins, *The Professor's House*, came out in 1925. Cather's hero, Tom Outland, lamented the fact that "we had only a small Kodak, and these pictures didn't make much show—

looked, indeed, like scrubby little 'dobe ruins such as one can find almost anywhere. They gave no idea of the beauty and vastness of the setting." Gilpin thought her pictures of the majestic, sculptural ruins compensated for Outland's shortcomings. Some of Cather's writings even seemed to describe her own photographs. "Far above me," Cather had written, "a thousand feet or so, set in a great cavern in the face of the cliff, I saw a little city of stone, asleep. It was still as sculpture—and something like that. It all hung together, seemed to have a kind of composition." Gilpin hoped to interest Cather in collaborating on an illustrated edition of *The Professor's House*; unfortunately, her efforts to contact the author failed.

Laura Gilpin self-published her Mesa Verde photographs in 1927 in the book *The Mesa Verde National Park: Reproductions from a Series of Photographs by Laura Gilpin*.

Laura first encountered the subject that was to dominate the rest of her artistic life in 1930. While driving on the Navajo Indian reservation in remote southwestern New Mexico with her friend Elizabeth Forster, Laura ran out of gas. Laura, always a sturdy traveler, hiked more than 10 miles to the nearest trading post to get more fuel. When she returned, she found her friend playing rummy with a group of Navajo Indians who had arrived to keep her company. A lifelong kinship between Laura and the Navajos was born in that moment, and throughout the rest of her life, Laura photographed the Navajos, lovingly creating an intelligent and compassionate record of a beleaguered Pueblo culture.

In 1930 she was elected an associate of the Royal Photographic Society of Great Britain, and in that same year the Library of Congress purchased a small collection of her photographs, but the Depression threatened the survival of her tiny gallery, and she was forced to focus on earning money. Laura published her own postcards and lantern slides and, in 1941, her first major book, *The Pueblos: A Camera Chronicle*. In the text of this book, Gilpin expressed her reverence for the ancient history of the Southwest, which was as "old as Egypt." Laura felt a connection with the rich history of the Pueblo and claimed it as her own. "There is something infinitely appealing in this land which contains our oldest history," she wrote, "something which once known will linger in one's memory with a haunting tenacity."

The photographs were a critical but not a financial success, and so, during the Second World War, Laura worked part-time as a photographer for Boeing to make ends meet. After the war she resettled in Santa Fe. In 1948 she published *Temples in the Yucatán: A Camera Chronicle of Chichen Itza*.

Laura's next book, *The Rio Grande: River of Destiny*, published in 1949, introduced a more mature and self-confident Laura Gilpin to the world. She placed a much greater emphasis, in this book, on cultural geography, a theme that was to also dominate the rest of her creative life.

Laura began work on the Rio Grande book in 1945, and during the next four years, she traveled more than 27,000 miles on borrowed gas ration coupons to make photographs for this ambitious project. Because the region was largely inaccessible by car, Laura packed in on horseback to photograph the river's source in Colorado, and she chartered a small plane to fly her over the river's confluence with the Gulf of Mexico. Author Martha Sandweiss describes Laura's book this way:

> Her plan for the book dictated the content of her pictures: The people—the Spanish Americans, the Mexicans and the Anglos are important but are

"The ladder, Acoma pueblo," photo by Laura Gilpin

subservient to the river. The people come and go—the river flows on forever. Thus she made few portraits, focusing instead on landscapes and pictures that showed the people in the context of their environment. She organized the book geographically, following the river down through the Colorado mountains and the fertile San Luis Valley, into the Indian and Hispanic regions of northern New Mexico, and out through the ranching areas of west Texas and the Mexican borderlands.

John Brinkerhoff Jackson, himself a student of the American landscape, reviewed the book as a "human geographical study," noting that Gilpin,

> has seen the river from its source to its end and permits us to see it through her eyes, not merely as a photogenic natural phenomenon, but as a force that has created a whole pattern of living, that has created farms and villages and towns and that continues to foster their growth. . . . Miss Gilpin is undoubtedly the first photographer to introduce us to the pueblos, the Spanish-American communities, the whole countryside of farms, as something more than picturesque.

Laura's interest in cultural context, though less prominent in her photographs, was now expressed in text. She lovingly describes the region in human terms, citing the river's mineral wealth, its use in growing food and nurturing livestock, and its value as an oasis for weary travelers looking for a place to settle.

The final page of the book, featuring a picture called "Rio Grande Yields Its Surplus to the Sea (1947)," makes an evocative statement, in text and image, about Laura Gilpin's feelings regarding the beauty and fragility of the relationship between humanity and the natural world. The text reads:

> Since the earliest-known existence of human life in the Western world, all manner of men have trod the river's banks. With his progressing knowledge and experience, man has turned these life-giving waters upon the soil, magically evoking an increasing bounty from the arid land. But through misuse of its vast drainage area—the denuding of forest lands and the destruction of soil-binding grasses—the volume of the river has been diminished, as once generous tributaries have become parched arroyos. Will present and future generations have the vision and wisdom to correct these abuses, protect this heritage, and permit a mighty river to fulfill its highest destiny?

Almost immediately upon finishing *The Rio Grande: River of Destiny*, Laura returned to the Navajo reservation with Elizabeth Forster, resolved to do another book on Navajo life. This time she wanted to emphasize Navajo tradition and cultural continuity, so she rephotographed many of the people that she had photographed years before, paying special attention to those who had preserved their ancient culture. She organized her book into four sections, corresponding to the importance of the number four in the Navajo religion. Laura wanted the book, which would be called *The Enduring Navaho*, to be written and photographed from a purely Navajo perspective.

The Navajo considered themselves the Dinéh, "the People of the Earth." As Laura wrote, they moved about in loneliness, though never lonely, in dignity and happiness, with song in their heart and on their lips, in harmony with the great forces of nature. The two salient qualities of the people were their dignity and their happiness. Both spring from their vital traditional faith, faith in nature, faith in themselves as a part of nature, faith in their place in the universe, deep-rooted faith born of their Oriental origin, molded and strengthened by the land in which they live.

The most important theme at work in *The Enduring Navaho* is the word *enduring*. Laura, like Elsie Clews Parsons, believed that Pueblo culture was alive and thriving in constant combination with new influences—remaining connected to the past, yet moving forward.

In 1972 Laura Gilpin published a book on the Canyon de Chelly. She was eighty-one years old. In this book she closely followed the lives of a small number of Navajo families that live in this New Mexico canyon, which is accessible only on horseback, led by a Navajo guide.

Laura Gilpin created a pictorial portrait of the entire historical and geological landscape of the Southwest. As Martha Sandweiss put it, Gilpin communicated

a landscape with a past measured not just in geological or evolutionary time but in human time, as evidenced by architectural ruins, ancient trails, and living settlements. It was a landscape with intrinsic beauty, but one whose greatest meaning derived from its potential to change and be changed by humankind. Gilpin did not dislike the idea of a wilderness, but for her there was no true wilderness in the Southwest, no area that had remained untouched by more than a thousand years of human settlement.

Laura never considered herself an artist. She was simply a photographer, who, for more than a half a century, practiced her profession with consummate craftsmanship and a great love for the world she captured with her camera.

Laura Gilpin knew that the Southwest sometimes provided a nurturing landscape, sometimes a hostile one. She knew that the landscape could be modified by human action, but she also believed that the landscape should and would remain the dominant force shaping and molding human culture.

MILLICENT ROGERS
1902–1953

Collector/Artist of Lifestyle

*T*he Sangre de Cristo Mountains swept across the brilliant blue southwestern sky like a painted dream as Standard Oil heiress Millicent Rogers made her way through Taos for the very first time, heading toward Mabel Dodge Luhan's Big House.

Like Millicent, Mabel was a transplanted East Coast heiress and a well-known hostess of literary and philosophical salons. Mabel had invited Millicent to her home as she had invited many of the best thinkers, artists, and collectors of her day. It was her hope that they would stay in Taos and help her create an oasis of enlightenment in the Enchanted Circle and preserve the Pueblo culture that dwelled at the heart of Mabel's vision.

Mabel knew that Millicent would be a great addition to her new community and would do much to enhance and popularize the region. Millicent was a trendsetter and collector who moved in the most rarefied of circles. Her daring taste influenced many of her contemporaries, and she was blessed with an impeccable eye for style and quality. She also had a keen intelligence that Mabel suspected would allow her to understand and appreciate the unique beauty of Native American arts and crafts and, in turn, help convince the world that these treasures were worth preserving.

An aesthetic kinship was immediately apparent to Millicent when she entered Mabel's house. The great room where Mabel greeted Millicent was a spacious and airy chamber that opened to the sweeping southwestern desert. It was crowned with massive aspen-wood "vigas," or beams, that lent a rustic elegance to the surroundings. The dining room was patterned after Mabel's famous Italian villa, with an ornate chandelier and precious silver wall sconces. Contrasting this old-world grandeur was the room's rough-hewn ceiling, finished with mud, scented with sage, and painted with earthy pigments in a pattern resembling a Navajo weaving. Never had Millicent seen simplicity and sophistication so harmoniously coupled.

And then there was Mabel herself in her voluminous Indian robes with her hair upswept, a living symbol of Gilded Age sophistication taking on the trappings of a new world. Tony Luhan, Mabel's husband, loomed like a silent and enduring spirit of the pueblos by her side. Millicent knew in that moment that she had found a new home and a new mission.

Millicent's son, Paul Peralta-Ramos, remembers that first encounter with Mabel and Tony as a meeting filled with mysticism and new discovery: "There was Tony in a white sheet, looking like a pope, and sitting on one of Mabel's Florentine chairs from Italy. He looked very pontifical and I was ready to bow and kiss his ring or something like that."

As was characteristic of an evening at Mabel's, Millicent experienced a poetic introduction to a lyrical land, and a few months later, Millicent moved to New Mexico. She set up residence in a hotel in Taos while construction on her home was completed.

She and her son Paul went on extended treks into the heart of Pueblo country. They watched ancient ceremonial dances on the pueblos and began to gather what was to become one of the world's most impressive collections of Native American arts and crafts. These artifacts would later provide the seed collection for the Millicent Rogers Museum. The museum is an institution that to this day carries on Millicent's mission to preserve and display the beauty of a vanishing American Southwest.

The barren and rustic expanses of Taos, New Mexico, might seem an odd place to find a Standard Oil heiress, but Millicent Rogers had never been your average debutante. She had never been a run-of-the-mill anything, and when we look at her past and her unique origins, we can begin to understand why she chose Taos as her final home and her final and most heartfelt preservation project.

Millicent Rogers was born in 1902. She was the granddaughter of Henry Huttleston Rogers, a partner of John D. Rockefeller's in the Standard Oil Company, and the driving force behind Anaconda Copper and U.S. Steel. Thanks to the independence of his spirit and the originality of his mind, Henry Huttleston Rogers became very wealthy, and when he died, he left an estate of more than $150 million to his son, Millicent's father, Colonel Henry Rogers.

So from her very earliest beginnings, Millicent lived in a world of opulence and lavish comfort. She was used to the finest things in life. But she inherited more from her grandfather than his spectacular fortune. Millicent also inherited his quick intelligence and driving energy. These made her stand apart from the rest of the young women in her privileged social circle.

Millicent's mother, Mary Benjamin Rogers, was the daughter of Park Benjamin, a prominent New York journalist and poet. It was most probably from this side of the family that Millicent inherited her keen intellect and her artistic sensitivity.

Millicent contracted rheumatic fever when she was just eight years old, and that illness changed her life forever. Her health was fragile from that day forward. As a consequence she developed a thirst for living in the moment and an awareness that life was short and unpredictable. This gave her the courage to push the envelope of social acceptability at times as well as a dedication to alleviate the suffering of others. Millicent Rogers was a woman of exceptional warmth, humor, and understanding. After the Second World War, she raised more than $1 million for medical supplies to go to Europe and Asia.

Even in the height of the opulent Jazz Age, when individuality was encouraged, Millicent was considered extravagant and unusual. She was a willowy, statuesque, strikingly beautiful young woman who had learned a love and flair for fashion from her mother. But Millicent went beyond following the trends of haute couture and worked hand in hand with the designers of her day to create her own unique style.

Millicent adored costumes and playing special roles. Everywhere she went she found new inspiration. In her house on the St. James River, she had a fashion designer named Mainbocher make her dresses in the period of Louis Philippe. In the Austrian valley of the Arlberg Mountains, where she had a house filled with superb Biedermeier furniture, she wore Tyrolean hats. She would have the village tailor from Innsbruck, Austria, make her authentic peasant aprons, scarves, jackets, and vests, and she would combine these with Provençal quilted skirts and peasant blouses or pullover sweaters by Schiaparelli. And at one ball welcoming the Prince of Wales, she set off her simple black velvet dress with an ornate headdress from Chinatown. It is said that the prince had eyes only for Millicent that night!

Millicent had many celebrated suitors, including Clark Gable, Roald Dahl, and Ian Fleming, but marriage did not seem to agree with her. Millicent settled on the first of her three husbands in 1924. She married Count Ludwig Salm von Hoogstraeten, a former Austrian cavalryman and, soon after, gave birth to the first of her three sons, Peter Salm.

Millicent and the Count divorced in 1927, and Millicent married Arturo Peralta-Ramos, the scion of a wealthy Argentine family whose chief passions in life were cars and racing bobsleds. The couple had two sons, Arturo and Paul, and divorced in 1935. Millicent married Ronald Balcom in 1936. Balcom was a financier and champion skier, but that marriage also failed after only five years. Her youngest son, Paul, had the following to say about Millicent's unsuccessful career as a wife: "The Count was a nice guy. They couldn't get along. My father was a nice guy. They couldn't get along. As for Ronnie Balcom, he was a really nice guy. They couldn't get along."

In 1947 Millicent moved to Taos, New Mexico. She had been living in California with her friend actress Janet Gaynor and Janet's husband, the designer Adrian. On their first trip to New Mexico, the trio stayed at a friend's ranch near Santa Fe, but after seeing Mabel Dodge Luhan's home, Millicent resolved to settle in Taos.

When Millicent arrived to take up residence in a hotel while overseeing the building of an adobe home, the tiny village of Taos was abuzz with the arrival of this social doyenne. She and her son Paul scouted the terrain, absorbing every detail of the southwestern landscape and immersing themselves in the rich cultural heritage of the region.

While in Navajo land, Millicent purchased the finest weavings; while in Acoma and Hopi land, the finest pottery and jewelry; and from the Spanish she bought religious santos, retablos, and other artifacts.

She moved into her rambling adobe house in 1949. She could often be seen moving about the house barefoot in Indian skirts and blouses and massive turquoise and silver bracelets and necklaces. As was her usual habit, every aspect of her life, including her clothing, reflected her newfound style and mission.

Feeling a deep sensitivity with the struggling Pueblo cultures, Millicent began working for Indian rights with Frank Waters, author of *The Man Who Killed the Deer*. Together they worked toward the formation of more humane policies to govern America's affairs with New Mexico's seven northern Pueblos.

Millicent's health, which had been fragile since her bout with rheumatic fever, began to falter, and she spent increasing amounts of time in her home. Her favorite place to convalesce was in her tranquil, sunlit bedroom, which had become her final salon. It was an airy, oversized room with comfortable couches and chairs. Her family, friends, and favorite art surrounded her. Here she began to create jewelry, drawing inspiration from the metals, minerals, and mythology of the region and her own inimitable sense of symmetry and style. Paul, who spent the most time with Millicent toward the end of her life, paints a peaceful and cheerful portrait of that time:

> The family would sit around, read magazines and talk. It was never considered a sickroom. She'd been ill almost all of her life, and both she and the rest of us knew it and took it for granted. At one point she suffered a stroke on her left side and she made herself work on her jewelry, dealing with large hunks of metal, and using the wax technique, which entailed her pushing the metal into the wax with all her strength. Eventually, there were little or no side effects from the stroke.

Millicent had a series of small strokes, and on January 1, 1953, she died of a massive stroke at the age of fifty. Paul said: "It would take something like that to do in M-R. She didn't believe in limitations, and time was her only true enemy."

But Paul found a way to let Millicent, finally, conquer her enemy once and for all. After her death Paul founded the Millicent Rogers Museum to display Millicent's magnificent collection of southwestern art and artifacts to the public, thus giving the gift of immortality to Millicent's incomparable sense of style.

Paul gives the following reasons for opening the museum:

> I'd been collecting along with her. I bought it from the estate and it was really a joke—the lawyer, who knew nothing about Southwestern artifacts and jewelry, said, "What are we going to do with all this junk?" That really irritated me. I'd been driving M-R to all the pueblos and reservations from the time I was 19 and I was living here and it was a part of my life too.

The museum first opened in temporary quarters on Ledoux Street in Taos in the mid-1950s. In the late 1960s, the museum moved into its present home, a house built by Claude J. K. and Elizabeth Anderson and later donated to the museum. The building was renovated and expanded in the mid-1980s by renowned architect Nathaniel A. Owings, founder of the architecture firm Skidmore, Owings, & Merrill LLP.

To Millicent Rogers the arts—southwestern jewelry and textiles in particular—expressed the spirit of the place and people. To Millicent each piece in her collection was a delicate survivor of an ancient world being threatened with extinction by an increasingly industrialized and Anglo world. She believed in preserving these cultural treasures and the spirit that produced them for generations to come. In an era when very few saw the value or beauty of Indian culture, Millicent collected and preserved a sampling of it, anticipating a time when America could appreciate the beauty of its own heritage.

JESUSITA ARAGON
1908–

La Partera: Healer and Midwife

Fourteen-year-old Jesusita Aragon was out with the sheep on her family's ranch in Trujillo, New Mexico, when she saw her sister running across the field to find her. Her sister had come to tell her that her Aunt Petra was going into labor, and their grandmother, who was a midwife, was 40 miles away delivering a baby for another woman.

Jesusita told her sister to watch over the sheep and ran back toward the house to help her aunt. When their grandmother returned the next morning, she asked about Petra and was told that Jesusita had delivered Petra's baby and that mother and baby were just fine. Jesusita's grandmother beamed and said, "That's good." From that day forward Jesusita worked at her grandmother's side, teaching her hands and her heart the fundamental skills of healing and midwifery, preparing for the day when she too would be La Partera.

"Parteras" or "curanderas" were women healers and midwives, who practiced a folk medicine brought to this removed part of the country by their Mexican ancestors. Their philosophy stressed a harmony with God and the natural world and was a blend of religious ritual and traditional healing methods. Herbal teas, poultices, and purgatives, as well as prayers and appeals to favorite saints, were common remedies. Because of the extreme geographical and cultural isolation of this region, and the poverty, there was no access to western doctors and hospitals. Parteras provided the only medical attention that these people knew. When a woman was ready to give birth, she called La Partera to come and help her deliver.

It was into this tradition that Jesusita's grandmother initiated her young granddaughter, and Jesusita eventually became a partera in her own right. Jesusita Aragon had delivered more than 12,000 babies by 1980. She also built a small maternity center, including the building and the furnishings, completely by hand. Here she cared for the young mothers and children of her community, many of whom could not turn to husbands or families for help.

For many years Jesusita Aragon has provided the people of northeastern New Mexico, many of whom were living in frontier conditions only a few decades ago, with their only source of comfort and healing. Jesusita is a living bridge between a tradition of female healers and western medicine. She worked in conjunction with doctors and hospitals, teaching them the wisdom she had gained through her many years healing the sick and delivering babies and ensuring that the women and children of her community stayed healthy and happy.

Jesusita Aragon was born in a tiny New Mexican mountain town outside Las Vegas in 1908. The family moved to nearby Trujillo when Jesusita was three. Jesusita was one of eight children, all girls, only three of whom survived to adulthood. Her family, like most of the families in the area, were subsistence farmers. Men, women, and children worked hard outside all day long to provide for themselves and one another. The land was often parched or frozen in this high-country desert, and people and animals were vulnerable to the region's severe weather changes. Travel in and out of the region was difficult, and medical attention and supplies were scarce. Five of Jesusita's sisters died before the age of six.

When construction began on the Storrie Dam, Jesusita's father got a job on the construction crew and moved his family to Las Vegas, New Mexico. With a little more money coming in, things got a little easier until Jesusita was ten. Then, in 1918, a bad flu epidemic swept through northern New Mexico felling many people, young and old, including Jesusita's mother, Antonia, and her new baby sister. So from the very beginning, the health of mothers and children was a central and defining issue in Jesusita's life.

> My mother was pregnant when she got sick. And she last three days, and couldn't talk no more. She start with a pain on her back, and it come through her chest so she couldn't talk. She writes to my grandmother when she wants something. And her tears run. I cry and she cries. I was scared, and I stayed with her. She was about seven months with the baby. The doctor took care of her and said it was better for her to have the baby than to die with the baby in because she was not going to last too long. And the doctor gave her something to make her have the baby. . . . My grandmother delivered it by herself, nobody was with her, just the neighbors, right here in Upper Town. It was another girl, the last one. I heard that baby cry. The baby girl last about an hour, I think, then she die. I think my mother didn't feel anything; she was so sick. And in a few days my mother die. She was thirty-four.

After Antonia's death the family moved back to Trujillo and ranch life. Jesusita, who was the oldest child in the family, helped her grandmother and aunts cook the meals and take care of the home and family. Jesusita also did a lot of work outside around the ranch, helping her father. Jesusita often said that her father called her "amigo" because he was expecting her to be a boy, so she worked outdoors the way an eldest son would. She followed behind the horses, spreading seed or gathering the crops at harvest time, and sheared the sheep in spring and even helped take the wool to market.

Jesusita also helped out with the animals on the ranch. She herded sheep and goats, which was no small task, as the family had 2,000 sheep and 500 goats, as well as cows and pigs. Often Jesusita would be deep into the foothills watering the sheep when a storm would blow in. Then she would have to spend the night alone with the sheep until the weather cleared and she could lead the sheep, and herself, safely home.

> When it rained and I was out far with the sheeps I have to stay there, taking care of them. I get under a rock or under a good tree. Sometimes I'm scared. Real scared. I cry and pray and have my dogs, one on one side and the other on the other side. . . . The sheep and goats go under trees when we have a big storm. And when we have a big hail sometimes it hurts them. Or kill them if it's a big one, and it hits them on the head. We used to lost too many sometimes.

Jesusita learned how to ride a horse, shoot a gun, and how to spot rattlesnakes at twenty paces away. She also learned how to nurse animals that were wounded, or sick, or in labor. Jesusita demonstrated a skill and compassion far beyond her years when caring for her family's animals, and the word spread. Soon, when anyone in the surrounding area had an animal that needed medical attention, they would call for Jesusita to come and nurse it back to health or help it deliver young.

> After I'm older sometimes the neighbors have trouble with their animals, and they come to ask me for help. One of my neighbors, he has too many problems with his goats and sheep. One goat is born with no front legs, and one set of twins are born dead. So I tell him how to change; to change the males with some other neighbor, so he can get good sheep and goats. I teach him how to breed.

Jesusita's only luxury during these years was dancing. Jesusita learned to dance at a village fiesta when she was twelve years old, and her love of dancing has continued to this day, although she is well into her nineties. She remembered her first dance this way:

> Also, I learn to dance, and I love to dance, then and now. They teach me in the house, my grandfather, my uncles, my daddy, everybody teach me how to dance. The first dance I went to when I was twelve years old. I remember it well, and I dance there with everybody. Gregario Parson and my uncles play the music. We had all kinds of tunes, all kinds. They used to play cuadrillas, like square dances, and waltzes, polkas. . . . I especially like to waltz.

Jesusita turned out to be a skilled and passionate dancer. Even when she was working with the sheep in the hills far from home, she would race back to town on her horse and go straight to the dances in her jeans and work shirt. No one bothered her about her clothing, however. Everyone was always happy to see Jesusita dance, no matter what she was wearing.

Jesusita also loved school, and she became the first and only person in her home, and one of the few in her village, who spoke English. And so Jesusita took on another role in the village—that of interpreter. She was regularly called whenever travelers got lost in the village and needed directions.

Jesusita enjoyed learning. She was a quick study and dreamed of becoming a nurse, but girls weren't educated after the eighth grade, so Jesusita's formal education came to an end when she was only thirteen years old. Also at that time Jesusita's father married again, and there was little love or affection between Jesusita and her new stepmother. Jesusita, therefore, turned to her grandparents and spent more and more time by her grandmother's side, learning to become a partera who needed no other education than her firsthand experience.

> But my grandmother used to tell me everything. She teach me everything, and I like to hear what is this or that and that and that. So I learn. I don't know why, but I always said that I'm going to be a midwife, and she used to tell me, "Yeah, you better be, because when I die you're going to be the one that takes care of everybody. . . ." And that was true.

Trouble began for Jesusita when she became pregnant out of wedlock at twenty-three years of age. Her boyfriend refused to marry her, and her father and grandmother, upon whom she depended for support and love, were furious with her. She was turned out of the house, and they even refused to feed her after a hard day's work. She wasn't allowed to go to mass anymore, and, perhaps hardest of all to bear, she wasn't allowed to go to the village dances anymore.

Jesusita gave birth to an eleven-pound baby boy, whom she named Ernesto. Her grandmother delivered her baby, but Jesusita wasn't given the normal period of rest afforded most new mothers. "When I have Ernesto my family didn't care about me. . . . They make me get up, and they send me out. 'You can go work, you can do this, you can do that,' they say to me. They make me go out in the rain and work like usual, and they didn't care about me. I'm sorry to tell you that, but that the way I go."

So once again Jesusita was affected in a very personal way by the lack of proper care and support for new mothers and children. Events like these surely must have fueled her determination even further to ensure that no new mother or child would have to go without the care that they required.

Jesusita retreated from village and family life during those years. Her family barely spoke to her. A social worker came to her occasionally with clothes for Jesusita and the baby, but this was all the help and support she received. She stayed alone with her new son and felt ashamed and asked God to take her, because she wanted to die.

But Jesusita's prayers went unanswered, and she decided that God wanted her on earth for a reason. Jesusita gathered up her strength and reentered village life, determined to find a place in the world. Her first act of defiance was to go to the very next dance in her village.

> So I went to the dance, and my grandmother was real mad. But I went to the dance. . . . I went in, and I started dancing the same thing like before my baby. And people didn't ask me anything. They didn't say, "Why did you not come? I heard that you had a baby." No. Nobody

asked me nothing. Oh, they were just so glad to see me. They liked me. It's a good memory. Real good.

Jesusita got pregnant a second time and gave birth to a baby daughter, Dolores. Her family was not willing to forgive this second pregnancy, and her grandmother, who had helped so many strangers, left her own granddaughter to have her baby alone. But Jesusita, used to taking care of herself, laid out everything the way her grandmother had taught her and delivered her own baby. She decided then that that was it. She would have no more babies, but she would help others to have an easier time than she had experienced.

Jesusita lived in Trujillo with her children until Ernesto was ready for high school. She was committed to ensuring that Ernesto and Dolores, and her nephew Ben, whom Jesusita was raising after the death of her sister, would have the chance that she never had. She wanted them all to go to high school. So in 1952 Jesusita moved to Las Vegas and washed and ironed and cleaned houses so that her children could afford to go to school. She later got a job in a parachute factory. In her spare time she delivered babies, dividing her time between her job at the factory and midwifery.

Fortunately, Jesusita had an understanding boss at the parachute factory, and he would excuse her absences when she had to travel many miles to help a woman in need. But gradually it became apparent to Jesusita that the best service she could offer to her patients, many of whom were in trouble at home, was a maternity center where they could come and have their babies in a peaceful and supportive environment. And the best thing she could do for herself and her children was to build them a home.

Jesusita saved up enough money to buy a small parcel of land in Las Vegas, and brick by brick, she built herself a house with her own two hands. Her helpers were her neighbors, friends, and relatives, mostly women who demonstrated the determination, resilience, and strength that the women who lived in Jesusita's region were known for.

> I did lots back then. While I was working at the parachute factory I get ready to build my house, the house I live in now. I was working there, and then when we get off, about four o'clock or four thirty, I come here and work on my house. When it gets dark I build a fire, so I can see to work. There wasn't nothing here then, no electricity, no water. So I and Julia, my friend, and Mrs. Duran, my neighbor, we get together, the three of us, and we go to the electric plant and ask for light. They say, "Yes, we give it to you if you dig the big holes for the poles, because we are too busy to dig them." So Ben and one of my nieces, Agapeta Trujillo, dig my two holes for me, and Julia paid them to dig the two for her, and Mrs. Duran paid them, too. So in about three days we have light here. You know, the men, they won't do anything. They say "Oh, no, you won't get anything." But they don't care, but we women do it. We try it and do it. Sometimes women do things better than them, better than men.

Jesusita began to deliver babies in her new home/maternity center and spent her time caring for young mothers, many of whom, like Jesusita herself, had been put out by their families and had nowhere else to turn. She cared for the sick and the spurned, the lonely and the frightened, and she brought comfort and safety to so many others.

Jesusita not only cared for the sick and delivered babies, but she also arranged adoptions for the unplanned babies of university students, counseled women who had a hard time caring for their children, and so as not to waste one square foot of her precious resource, Jesusita offered her maternity center as a halfway house for patients from a nearby psychiatric hospital. And to this day Jesusita has never charged more than $50 for maternity services that often span the entire length of the pregnancy.

In the old days, when a woman breeched or other complications arose, Jesusita would deliver the babies herself. And although the circumstances would seem very unfamiliar indeed to women who have given birth in a traditional western hospital, Jesusita had a very good record for delivering healthy babies and women.

Jesusita often delivered babies in the old-fashioned way, with women crouching on the floor and holding onto a rope that was tied to the vigas, or ceiling beams, above to help her push. There were statues of saints arranged around the room, and hot water and binding cloths and olive oil to wash the babies in once they were born. And, most important, there were Jesusita's educated hands that simultaneously healed and comforted frightened women in the throes of labor. She could tell by a touch if a baby was positioned correctly and the womb was healthy or if there would be complications that required a doctor's care.

As access to hospitals improved, Jesusita began to work in tandem with doctors, sending them her difficult patients when she felt they needed the care that a hospital could provide. Jesusita would telephone the hospital to let them know what to expect when her patient arrived, and doctors and attendants always listened to her, because she always turned out to be right!

Jesusita is in her nineties now, and her house remains full of young mothers and children, as well as visitors from the surrounding region who knock day and night to ask Jesusita for advice and help. And Jesusita always gives her healing love and wisdom to everyone who needs it. "I always said when I was a little girl that I want to be a nurse or a midwife, but I didn't have the chance to be a nurse. I didn't finish my school, just the eighth grade. So, I be a midwife, and I like it. I'm so happy all the time. It doesn't bother me when they need me any time, day or night."

BIBLIOGRAPHY

Bryant, Keith L., Jr. *The History of the Atchison Topeka and Santa Fe Railway.* Lincoln: University of Nebraska Press, 1982.

Buss, Fran Leeper. *La Partera: Story of a Midwife.* Ann Arbor: University of Michigan Press, 1980.

Deacon, Desley. *Elsie Clews Parsons: Inventing Modern Life.* Chicago: University of Chicago Press, 1997.

Gilpin, Laura. *The Enduring Navaho.* Austin: University of Texas Press, 1968.

———. *The Pueblos: A Camera Chronicle.* New York: Hastings, 1942.

———. *The Rio Grande: River of Destiny.* New York: Duell, Sloan and Pearce, 1949.

Grattan, Virginia L. *Mary Colter, Builder Upon the Red Earth.* Grand Canyon, AZ: Grand Canyon Association, 1992.

Hurst, Tricia. "Heiress Brings Lavish Lifestyle to Taos." *New Mexico Magazine,* November 1989.

Jackson, Rosie. *Frieda Lawrence.* London: Rivers Oram Press, 1999.

Lawrence, Frieda. *Frieda Lawrence: The Memoirs and Correspondence.* New York: Alfred A. Knopf, 1964.

Luhan, Mabel Dodge. *Edge of the Taos Desert: An Escape to Reality.* Albuquerque: University of New Mexico Press, 1987.

Morris, Juddi. *The Harvey Girls: The Women Who Civilized the West.* Walker, 1994.

Rudnick, Lois Palken. *Mabel Dodge Luhan: New Woman New Worlds.* Albuquerque: University of New Mexico Press, 1984.

Sandweiss, Martha A. *Laura Gilpin: An Enduring Grace.* Fort Worth, TX: Amon Carter, 1986.

———. "Laura Gilpin and the Tradition of American Landscape Photography." Online. http://www.sla.purdue.edu/WAAW/Sandweiss/

BIBLIOGRAPHY

Weigle, Marta and Barbara A. Babcock. *The Great Southwest of the Fred Harvey Company and the Santa Fe Railway.* Tucson: University of Arizona Press, 1996.

ℐNDEX

A

Adams, Ansel, 64, 95

Alvarado Hotel, 26, 32–33

Aragon, Jesusita, 115–25
  birth of, 116
  childhood of, 118
  creation of maternity
    center, 123
  as a dancer, 119–20
  education of, 120
  as an interpreter, 120
  as a midwife, 115, 116, 122,
    124–25
  mother's death, 117
  pregnancies of, 120–21, 122
  as a veterinarian, 118–19

B

Billy the Kid, 7

Boas, Franz, 34–35

Brett, Dorothy, 67

Buffalo Bill, 19

C

Cather, Willa, 64

Chapel of Loretto, 1, 8

Clarence H. White School,
  99–100

Collier, John, 64

Colter, Mary, 23–33
  birth of, 25
  childhood of, 23
  as a designer for the Fred
    Harvey Company, 31–33
  education of, 25–26
  move to the Pacific
    Northwest, 29
  relationship with workers, 30
  retirement of, 33

curanderas. *See* parteras.

E

El Ortiz, 31

Evans, Bonnie, 68

F

Fewkes, Jesse W., 18–19

Fred Harvey Company, 25, 26,
  28–33, 45–55

G

Gallery 291, 84, 86

Geronimo, 19

Gilpin, Laura, 64, 94–107
  background of, 98–99
  birth of, 98
  education of, 99
  first encounter with Navajo
    Indians, 101

interest in cultural context,
104–5
publication of *The Enduring
Navaho*, 105–6
publication of *The Mesa Verde
National Park: Reproductions from
a Series of Photographs by Laura
Gilpin*, 101
publication of *The Pueblos: A
Camera Chronicle*, 102
publication of *The Rio Grande:
River of Destiny*, 102
publication of *Temples in the
Yucatán: A Camera Chronicle of
Chichen Itza*, 102

Grand Canyon National
Park, 19

H

Harvey Girl Museum, The, 49

Harvey Girls, The, 45–55
advertisement for, 45
background of, 47
as college students, 48
compensation for, 49
description of, 52
guidelines for, 49
legacy of, 55

*Harvey Girls: The Women Who Civilized
the West, The*, 48

Harvey Way, 49

Harvey, Fred, 20, 45, 50–52

Hemenway Archeological
Expedition, 18

Hermits Rest, 32

Hopi House, 20, 28–29

Hopi Indians, 35–37

Hopi pottery, 12, 15–16, 17

L

La Fonda, 53–54

Lamy, John Baptist, 3

landscape photography,
95–96

Lawrence, D. H., 64–65, 69–70,
75, 77

Lawrence, Frieda, 65, 69–77
autobiography, *Frieda Lawrence,
the Memoirs and Correspondence*,
77
description of, 72
divorce from Ernest
Weekley, 74
family history of, 72
first visit to Taos, 75
friendship with Mabel Dodge
Luhan, 75
as an inspiration for D. H.
Lawrence's writing, 77
marriage to Antonio Ravagli,
75, 77
marriage to Ernest Weekley,
69, 73
memoir, *Not I, but the Wind*, 77
relationship with D. H.
Lawrence, 69–70, 74

Luhan, Antonio, 62–63, 68

Luhan, Mabel Dodge, 19, 56–68,
  75, 90–91, 108–9
  as an advocate for the Pueblo
    Indians, 61
  affair with John Reed, 60
  as an avant-garde New York
    hostess, 60
  birth of, 57
  childhood of, 57
  civic contributions of, 67
  death of, 67–68
  development of an artist
    community, 64
  friendship with D. H. and
    Frieda Lawrence, 64–65
  as an Italian Renaissance
    hostess, 59
  marriage to Antonio Luhan, 62
  marriage to Karl Evans, 57, 59
  marriage to Maurice Sterne, 60
  memoir, Edge of the Taos Desert, 61
  move to Taos, 61
  psychic experiences of, 56,
    60–61, 63–64
  suicide attempts of, 59, 60

Luhan's Big House, 63, 108

M

Martinez, Maria, 78–83
  as an artist, 80
  birth of, 81
  children of, 82
  as a cultural preservationist, 80
  death of, 83
  discovery of a new form of
    pottery, 78
  first car of, 80–81

legacy of, 82–83
  marriage to Julian Martinez,
    81, 82
  pottery techniques of, 81–82

Mesa Verde, 100–101

Meyers Sisters, The, 48–49

Millicent Rogers Museum, The,
  110, 114

Mother Magdalen, 1–11
  civic involvement of, 10
  death of, 10

Mother Magdalen's Miracle
  Staircase, 1, 9–11

Mother Matilda, 3–4

N

Nampeyo, 12–22
  artistic legacy of, 12–13
  blindness of, 12, 20–21
  children of, 21
  death of, 21
  description of, 17
  family lineage of, 16–17, 22
  marriage to Lesso, 17
  national recognition of, 17

Native American Pottery, 78

Navajo Indians, 101, 105

O

O'Keeffe, Georgia, 64, 84–93
  artistic success of, 87–88
  birth of, 88
  as a commercial artist, 89

critics of, 87
death of, 92
early relationship with Alfred
    Stieglitz, 86
education of, 88–89
exhibits of, 90
first visit to Taos, 90
flower theme, 90
learning to drive, 91
marriage to Alfred Stieglitz, 87,
    91–92
move to New York City, 91
professional relationship with
    Alfred Stieglitz, 87
resurgence of popularity, 92
viewing her first public
    exhibit, 84

P

Parsons, Elsie Clews, 34–44
anthropological work of, 43
birth of, 38
childhood of, 39
courtship with Sam Dexter,
    39–40
death of, 43–44
education of, 40
family history of, 38–39
marriage to Herbert Parsons,
    40–41
publication of *Pueblo Indian
    Religion*, 38
research of Hopi Indians,
    35–37
sociological work of, 41–42
as a teacher, 41
as a writer, 41

parteras, 115–16

Peralta-Ramos, Paul. *See* Rogers,
    Millicent.

Phantom Ranch, 32

preservationists, 80

Pueblo Indian art, 20

Pueblo Indians, 34–35, 38

R

Rogers, Millicent, 108–14
birth of, 110
death of, 113
early marriages of, 111–12
family history of, 110
fashion of, 111
friendship with Mabel Dodge
    Lahun, 108–109
as an Indian rights activist, 113
son Paul, 109, 112, 113–14

Roosevelt, Teddy, 19

S

San Ildefonso, 80, 82

Sandweiss, Martha, 102–4, 106–7

Santa Fe Railroad, 20, 31, 45,
    47, 51

Sells, Opal, 47

Sioux Indians, 23

Sister Monica, 4

Sisters of Loretto, The, 1–11
history of, 3
journey westward of, 4–6

Sityatki Polychrome, 15

smallpox epidemic, 23

St. Paul, MN, 23

Stieglitz, Alfred, 84, 86, 91, 92

survey photographers, 97–98

W

Weekley, Ernest, 72–73